On Prayer

On Prayer

Conversation with God

John Calvin

Westminster John Knox Press
LOUISVILLE • LONDON

Scripture quotations, unless otherwise indicated, are from the New Revised Standard Version of the Bible, copyright © 1989 by the Division of Christian Education of the National Council of the Churches of Christ in the U.S.A., and used by permission.

"A Selection of Calvin's Prayers," pp. 38–43, is from I. John Hesselink, *Calvin's First Catechism: A Commentary,* Columbia Series in Reformed Theology (Louisville, KY: Westminster John Knox Press, 1997), 137–39.

Excerpt from *Calvin: Institutes of the Christian Religion* 3.20.1–20, 28–52; ed. John T. McNeill, trans. Ford Lewis Battles; 2 vols. Library of Christian Classics (Philadelphia: Westminster Press, 1960), 2:850–78, 888–920. All rights reserved.

Book design by Sharon Adams
Cover design by Eric Walljasper, Minneapolis, MN
Cover art: © Bettmann/Corbis

First edition
Published by Westminster John Knox Press
Louisville, Kentucky

This book is printed on acid-free paper that meets the American National Standards Institute Z39.48 standard. ∞

PRINTED IN THE UNITED STATES OF AMERICA

06 07 08 09 10 11 12 13 14 15— 10 9 8 7 6 5 4 3 2 1

Library of Congress Cataloging-in-Publication Data is on file at the Library of Congress, Washington, D.C.

ISBN-13: 978-0-664-23022-7
ISBN-10: 0-664-23022-9

Contents

Publisher's Note

Prayer is a central activity of Christian life. Both publicly and privately, Christians pray.

John Calvin (1509–1564), one of the leading Protestant reformers of the sixteenth century and an influential theologian whose insights into Scripture continue to provide nourishment for Christians, devoted one of the longest chapters in his *Institutes of the Christian Religion* to the topic of prayer. Book 3, chapter 20, of this work is divided into 52 sections in which Calvin discusses the nature and practice of prayer. Prayer was vital to Calvin's own Christian faith and he wanted to share his perceptions with others.

The topic of prayer is introduced by a veteran Calvin scholar, I. John Hesselink. His essay sets the chapter on prayer in the wider context of Calvin's theology as a whole and of his other writings on prayer.

The text of Calvin's chapter, reproduced here, is found with scholarly footnotes in the Library of Christian Classics edition, *Calvin: Institutes of the Christian Religion*, ed. John T. McNeill, trans. Ford Lewis Battles (Philadelphia:

Westminster Press, 1960). A polemical section of the chapter, on the intercession of saints, has been omitted here.

The size of Calvin's great work, the *Institutes*, is daunting. Only those interested in Calvin's theology as a whole tend to launch into this theological tome. The following presentation intends to make Calvin's chapter on prayer accessible to more people. It also features a short summary of the various sections of the work along with questions for reflection and discussion.

Our hope is that this volume will introduce a wider audience to Calvin's writings that nurture the church and Christian persons who continue to pray.

DONALD K. MCKIM
Westminster John Knox Press

Abbreviations

Comm. Commentary, indicates further comment on this
       verse or verses in Calvin's biblical commentaries
LXX   The Septuagint: Greek version of the Old Tes-
       tament
p   Paraphrase
Vg.   Vulgate version of the Bible

Introduction:
John Calvin on Prayer

I. John Hesselink

The two longest chapters in Calvin's *Institutes of the Christian Religion* (1559) are the chapter on faith and the chapter on prayer. Although it presupposes the larger context of Calvin's theology, the chapter on prayer can be read with understanding and profit even by those who know little or nothing about Calvin's thought. It is warm, practical, and pastoral, with only a few sections of a polemical nature (against the Roman Catholic view of the mediatorial intercession of saints). As the McNeill-Battles edition of the *Institutes* notes, "This thoughtful and ample chapter, with its tone of devout warmth, takes its place in the forefront of historically celebrated discussions of prayer."[1]

Yet, with few exceptions,[2] this gem has received little or no attention in the standard works on Calvin's life and thought. This is unfortunate because this chapter is an expression of the heart of Calvin's theology and his own personal piety. Udo Smidt is not exaggerating when he maintains that "the treatment and value given to prayer stand so dominantly at the center of Calvin's complete work that here the systematic theologian, the biblical scholar, the church teacher and the pastoral counselor all are speaking to us with equal force."[3]

This statement implies that one cannot have a complete appreciation of Calvin's understanding of prayer by relying solely on book 3, chapter 20 of the *Institutes*, valuable though that may be. Hence the purpose of this essay is to give a fuller picture of Calvin's doctrine of prayer by also citing passages from his catechisms, commentaries, and sermons. Calvin is not, as is sometimes imagined, a person of one book. Moreover, as will become apparent, Calvin's treatment of prayer, though very clear and easy to follow, is not all that simple, as alleged by T. H. L. Parker. He claims that "fundamentally, it is asking God for what we lack."[4] Rather, as Ronald Wallace concludes, for Calvin, "the heart and goal of prayer is communion with God."[5]

As indicated above, one can read Calvin's chapter on prayer as a self-standing entity without having a grasp of the whole of Calvin's theology. However, it should be noted that this chapter on prayer in the *Institutes* is near the conclusion of book 3, which deals with the place of faith as a work of the Holy Spirit. Note the title of book 3: "The Way in Which We Receive the Grace of Christ: What Benefits Come to Us from It, and What Effects Follow." The title of chapter 1 immediately indicates that this reception of the work of Christ is only possible because of the work of the Holy Spirit: "The Things Spoken Concerning Christ Profit Us by the Secret Working of the Spirit."[6] On the one hand, "faith is the principal work of the Holy Spirit" (*Inst.* 3.1.4); on the other hand, prayer is "the chief exercise (*praecipuum exercitium*) of faith."[7] Thus, as Calvin will emphasize again and again, true prayer is impossible apart from faith, stems from faith, and is a fruit of faith. In short, "we cannot pray to God without faith."[8]

One other matter needs to be touched on before proceeding to an exposition of Calvin's treatment of prayer, namely, the question of the development in his thought regarding this subject. In the case of some doctrines there are significant modifications or changes between the thought of the young Calvin who published the first (1536) edition of the *Institutes* at the age of twenty-seven and the final (1559) edition at the age of fifty (he died five years later). In the case of prayer, however, there are substantial additions to the first edition in the second (1539) edition, but many paragraphs from the first edition—and many statements in Calvin's first catechism—are repeated almost verbatim in the final edition.[9] The nature of this essay precludes a historical-critical comparison of the various editions, but one can get an idea of the development of Calvin's thought in regard to Calvin's exposition of the Lord's Prayer by examining Elsie Anne McKee's chapter on this subject in *The Lord's Prayer: Perspectives for Reclaiming Christian Prayer*, edited by Daniel L. Migliore.[10] She notes that the most significant additions to the 1539 edition are found in Calvin's commentary on the *Harmony of the Gospels* (1555). Many of these alterations are incorporated into the final edition of the *Institutes*.[11]

Five Presuppositions

1. God's gentle invitation

Calvin frequently refers to the fact that God commands us to pray, although the commands are usually accompanied by promises (*Inst.* 3.20.2, 14).[12] Commands to pray are found throughout Scripture. Calvin cites as examples Psalm 50:15 and Jesus' injunction in Matthew 7:7: "Seek and you will receive; knock, and it will be opened unto you." However, "a promise is here also added to the precept, as is necessary; for even though all admit that the precept ought to be obeyed, still the majority would flee from God when he calls if he did not promise to be easily entreated and readily accessible" (*Inst.* 3.20.13). "The Lord's precepts . . . are not destitute of his promise—two things that always hold the chief place in prayer" (3.20.24).

However, even given the fact that God demands that we pray and encourages us with many promises, it would be presumptuous and rash to approach the heavenly Father if he did not graciously and kindly invite us to pray. For

> until God has called us, we cannot come to him without being guilty of too much impudence and daring. Is it not folly and rashness for mortals to presume to address God? Therefore, we must wait until God calls us, which he does by his Word. For when he promises to be our Saviour he shows that he will always be ready to receive us. He does not wait till we come seeking him; rather, he offers himself and exhorts us to pray to him—and in doing so, tests our faith.[13]

Two things are suggested here. The one is that God takes the initiative in prayer. Although there are countless passages in Scripture where we are urged, if not commanded, to pray, "it would be rashness itself to burst into

God's sight if he himself had not anticipated our coming
by calling us" (*Inst.* 3.20.13). God does this through his
Word whereby he "makes himself familiar to us and opens
the door for us."[14] In a sermon on 2 Samuel 7:25–29,
Calvin translates a phrase in verse 29 to read, "For you, O
Lord of Hosts, God of Israel, have *opened the ear* of your
servant, saying . . ." (emphasis mine). Calvin then comments,

> We see that the point of these words is that we can-
> not pray to God with affection, and even that we are
> mute, until God opens our ears. For that opening of
> the ears opens our mouths as well. When we have
> heard God speak, then we respond mutually to him
> so that there is harmony and accord between his
> promises by which he draws himself to us, and those
> prayers by which we come to him.[15]

As we shall see later, God does this, that is, opens our ears,
by means of the Word and the Spirit, but here the emphasis is on God's gracious initiative, by which "we may taste
how gently God attracts us to himself" (*Inst.* 3.20.14).

That, as Calvin would say, is the first thing. The second is to note the gracious and loving character of this
God who invites us to pray. It is well known that Calvin
has an exalted view of the majesty of God, the supreme
ruler of the universe. What is not so well known is that
Calvin most frequently describes God the Redeemer in
terms of gratuitous mercy, love, and goodness and commonly speaks of God's "fatherly goodness" and "fatherly
love."[16]

If we were to think only of God's majesty and "formi-
dable presence," we would be awestruck and fearful and

hesitate to approach God in prayer. But when we are "persuaded of the exercise of God's paternal love toward us" and "his drawing near to us as a father,"[17] we are moved to address God in confidence in prayer. "For no one will ever rightly call upon God, unless he has a prior and certain trust in his goodness."[18]

2. Christ as Mediator and Intercessor

Closely related to the above is the fact that "Christ is constituted the only Mediator, by whose intercession the Father is for us rendered gracious and easily entreated" (*Inst.* 3.20.19). In this connection, Calvin refers to texts like 1 John 2:1, Romans 8:34 and 1 Timothy 2:5 which speak of Christ's role as advocate, intercessor, and mediator between God and humanity (3.20.20). "He alone bears to God the petitions of the people, who stay far off in the outer court" (ibid., an allusion to Heb. 9:24ff.). Because of our unworthiness we might hesitate to approach God with boldness and the confidence that our prayers will be answered, but with Christ as our intermediary "the throne of dreadful glory" is turned into "the throne of grace" (3.20.17; see Heb. 4:16). This was also true for believers prior to the coming of Christ. For "from the beginning, those who prayed were not heard save by the Mediator's grace." That was true not only for the saints under the old covenant. "We, too, "need a Mediator, who should appear in our name and bear us upon his shoulders and hold us bound upon his breast so that we are heard in his person" (*Inst.* 3.20.18). Calvin is adamant on this issue. He insists that "God can listen to no prayers without the intercession of Christ."[19] "No prayer is pleasing to God unless this Mediator [Christ] sanctifies it" (*Inst.* 3.20.27). "Let us learn to wash our prayers with the blood of our Lord Jesus Christ, for otherwise they shall be but profane and defiled."[20]

It is not too much to claim that everything that Calvin says about prayer revolves about the reconciling and intercessory work of Christ. Trusting in Christ as our mediator and advocate, we can approach God confidently and "intimately." Not only that, in a striking observation, Calvin suggests that when we pray in this way, "We pray, as it were, by his mouth, since Christ gives us entrance and audience and intercedes for us (Rom. 8:34)."[21] In John 16:26 concerning Jesus' saying, "On that day you will ask in my name," Calvin comments, "This is a remarkable passage, by which we are taught that we have the heart of God as soon as we place before him the name of his Son."[22]

3. The Indispensability of the Word

The third presupposition is that our prayers must be grounded in, shaped by, and led by the Word. Citing Psalm 44:21, which refers to spreading "out our hands to a strange god," Calvin sees here a warning against praying to anything but the true God who has revealed himself in his Word. For "only out of faith is God pleased to be called upon, and he expressly bids that prayers be conformed to the measure of his Word." Not only that, "faith grounded upon the Word is the mother of right prayer" (*Inst.* 3.20.27). Hence "it is an axiom that our prayers are faulty insofar as they are not founded on the Word."[23]

More specifically, as we have already noted in another context, proper prayer looks to the promises in particular and relies on them. "There is nothing more efficacious in our prayers than to set God's Word before us and then to found our supplications upon his promises, as if

God dictated to us out of his own mouth what we were to ask."[24] Again, "Unless the promises of God shine on us and invite us to prayer, no sincere prayer can ever be drawn from us."[25]

Calvin makes basically the same point in his comments on James 1:6: "Ask in faith, never doubting . . .":

> Prayer has its due order and method, and this is his first lesson. We are not able to pray unless the Word leads our way. Likewise, before we pray, we must believe. Our praying is a testimony that we look hopefully to God for the grace he has promised. A man who has no faith in the promises is praying in pretence.[26]

Calvin constantly warns about hypocrisy and unbelief in relation to prayer. Where these are present, prayer is empty and a mockery. "When God's word and celestial truth are despised, there is then neither any real prayer, nor any other religious exercise; for unbelief pollutes and contaminates whatever is otherwise in its nature sacred."[27] One finds a similar observation in one of Calvin's sermons on Isaiah 53. Again there is a close connection between the Word and faith.

> For it is certain that, if our prayers are not ruled according to the Word of God, they are trifling and God rejects them. Nor can they be made in faith unless the assurance comes from the same source— that is, from the truth of God.[28]

For Calvin, the book of Psalms provides the best means of praying according to the Word. Here he found an "anatomy of all the parts of the soul," for the psalmists "lay open all their inmost thoughts and affections" and also expose all our vices. "In short, calling upon God is one of the principal means of securing our safety, and a better and more unerring rule for guiding us in this exercise cannot be found elsewhere than in the psalms."[29]

Calvin comes close to suggesting that "we pray the psalms" as several contemporary writers have suggested, but he often identifies with David in these psalms, both in his struggles and in his gratitude for God's deliverances. He readily concedes that he "follows David at a great distance." Yet it has been of "great advantage" to him to behold in David "as in a mirror . . . an example for imitation." In short, "whatever may serve to encourage us when we are about to pray to God, is taught us in this book."[30]

4. The role of the Holy Spirit

It is not surprising that "the theologian of the Holy Spirit"[31] should indicate in so many ways how the ability to pray aright—or to pray at all—is made possible by the Holy Spirit. The obvious places for such discussions are those biblical passages that speak of the Holy Spirit in relation to prayer, for example, Romans 8:26: "Likewise the Spirit helps us in our weakness. For we do not know what to pray for as we ought, but the Spirit intercedes for us with groanings too deep for words." Calvin sees here a number of things. First, that "we are blind in praying to God" when we do so in our own power; for our "minds are too disturbed and confused to make the right choices." Second, the Spirit "must prescribe the manner of our praying," and third, the "Spirit affects our hearts in such a way that these prayers penetrate into heaven itself by their fervency." Granted, Jesus urges us to knock (Matt.

7:7), "but no one of his own accord could premeditate a single syllable, unless God were to knock to gain admission to our souls by the secret impulse of his Spirit, and thus open our hearts to himself."[32]

Calvin develops this point further in the *Institutes*. Because of our weakness, "God gives us the Spirit as our teacher in prayer." Concerning the phrase, the Spirit "intercedes for us with unspeakable groans" ("sighs too deep for words," Rom. 8:26 NRSV), Calvin explains: "Not that [the Spirit] actually prays or groans but arouses in us assurance, desires, and sighs, to conceive which our natural powers could scarcely suffice." "To pray rightly is a rare gift." Therefore, we need "the guidance of the Spirit" (*Inst.* 3.20.5).

> Hence, except one is guided by the Spirit of God, he cannot pray from the heart. And we know that it is the peculiar office of the Spirit to raise up our hearts to heaven; for we pray in vain unless we bring faith and repentance; and who is the author of these but the Holy Spirit?[33]

Calvin is aware of the fact that this emphasis on the Spirit might foster lethargy and passivity since the Holy Spirit is not at our beck and call. So he raises the issue in his catechism and asks, "Does the doctrine imply by this that we are to sit quiescent, and, as it were, lazily await the movement of the Spirit?" The answer, not surprisingly, is "Not at all. The meaning rather is that when the faithful feel cold and sluggish or somewhat indisposed to pray, they should forthwith flee to God and demand [!] that they be inflamed with the fiery darts of his Spirit, so as to be rendered fit for prayer."[34]

He mentions the same danger in the *Institutes* and puts the matter even more colorfully. Just because we are to rely on the aid of the Holy Spirit should not lead us to "vegetate in that carelessness to which we are all too prone" or "drowsily wait until [the Spirit] overtake our preoccupied minds. But rather, . . . loathing our inertia and dullness, we should seek such aid of the Spirit." Calvin then alludes to the apostle's exhortation to "pray in the Spirit" (1 Cor. 14:15). This indicates that reliance on the Spirit calls for "watchfulness" and also means that "the prompting of the Spirit empowers us so to compose prayers as by no means to hinder or hold back our own effort, since in this matter God's will is to test how effectually faith moves our hearts" (3.20.5). Here, as elsewhere, Calvin sees no conflict between the grace of the Spirit and human effort.

Calvin also refers frequently to Galatians 4:6: "God has sent the Spirit of his Son into our hearts, crying, 'Abba! Father!'" This not only assures us that we are children of God but also is the basis for our assurance and confidence in prayer. "Because the narrowness of our hearts cannot comprehend God's boundless favor, not only is Christ the pledge and guarantee of our adoption, but he gives the Spirit as witness to us of the same adoption, through whom with free and full voice we may cry 'Abba, Father' [Gal. 4:6; Rom. 8:15]. Therefore, whenever any hesitation shall hinder us, let us remember to ask him to correct our fearfulness, and to set before us that Spirit that he may guide us to pray boldly" (*Inst.* 3.20.37). So what the Spirit does, among other things, is to "pour confidence into our hearts so that we dare invoke God as our Father." Moreover, "since the confidence of our heart alone opens our mouth, our tongues will be dumb to utter prayers unless the Spirit bears testimony to our heart concerning the fatherly love of God."[35]

5. The importance of faith

In discussing the place of faith in regard to prayer, we should not regard it as a discrete subject, independent of the roles played by God's grace, Christ's intercession, the Word, and the work of the Holy Spirit. We have already seen how faith has been related in passing to the above themes. Note the interrelationships in Calvin's comments on James 1:6. "Prayer has its due order and method. . . . We are not able to pray unless the Word leads the way; likewise before we pray, we must believe. Our praying is a testimony that we look hopefully to God for the grace he has promised." The Holy Spirit is missing here but that is assumed. True faith, according to James, doubts nothing. So "faith which relies on the promises of God assures us that we shall receive what we ask for; consequently, it goes with a confidence and a certainty of the love God has for us."[36]

The inseparable relationship between faith and prayer is already evidenced in the title of the chapter on prayer in the *Institutes*, namely, "Prayer, Which Is the Chief Exercise of Faith, and by Which We Daily Receive God's Benefits."[37]

Based on several texts—Mark 11:24; Matthew 21:22, and James 1:5–7—Calvin sets forth what he believes is a basic principle: "Nothing is more in harmony with the nature of prayers than that this rule be laid down and established for them: that they not break forth by chance but follow faith as guide" (*Inst.* 3.20.11). Then, appealing to other New Testament texts, he simply concludes, "We can obtain nothing apart from faith" (ibid.).

The relationship between faith and prayer is reciprocal. On the one hand, "we cannot pray to God without faith."[38] Faith is "the source of prayer"[39] and "flows from faith."[40] Also, "our prayers are of no avail before God unless they are in some degree founded in faith, which alone reconciles us to God, since we can never be pleasing to God without pardon and remission of sins."[41]

On the other hand, prayer is a proof of our faith.[42] Without prayer, faith would become "languid and lifeless."[43] Again, "faith lies idle and even dead without prayer, in which the spirit of adoption shows and exercises itself, and by which we have evidence that all God's promises are considered by us as stable and sure."[44] Moreover, "our faith cannot be supported in a better way than by the exercise of prayer."[45] Calvin can even say that "prayer is raised upward by faith."[46]

Thus there is an inseparable relationship between faith and prayer. On the one hand, faith is the foundation and necessary condition of genuine prayer. On the other hand, prayer sustains and strengthens faith.[47] But it can also be put the other way around: faith is strengthened by prayer and prayer is nourished by faith. "The one then cannot be separated from the other, that is to say, that if we are resting upon the pledge of God's promises and have them thoroughly rooted in our hearts, we shall be stirred up to resort to God, so that our faith may exercise us in prayers and supplications."[48]

In the *Institutes* Calvin suggests six ways in which prayer contributes toward strengthening our faith:

> (1) it inflames our hearts with the desire to seek, love, and serve God; (2) it trains us to expose the secrets and desires of our hearts to God; (3) it promotes

gratitude; (4) it leads to meditation on God's kindness as a result of his having answered our prayers;
(5) it produces even greater joy in those things which
we have obtained through prayer; and (6) finally, it
serves as a personal confirmation of God's providence (3.20.3).[49]

The Meaning and Nature of Prayer

In a sense, the previous five points have all been prolegomena. Now we come to the nature of prayer itself.
Calvin has one fundamental definition of prayer, but in
the process of discussing prayer beyond the *Institutes* he
defines it in quite diverse ways. The brief and formal definition is that prayer is a "conversation" (3.20.4) or, more
particularly, "an intimate conversation" (*familiare alloquium*).[50] This sounds like a rather cozy way of describing
prayer, but Calvin cautions his readers against assuming
that this in any way denigrates the differences between the
creator and the creature. "Although prayer is an intimate
conversation of the pious with God, yet reverence and
moderation must be kept, lest we give loose rein to miscellaneous requests, and lest we crave more than God
allows; further that we should lift up our minds to a pure
and chaste veneration of him, lest God's majesty become
worthless for us" (3.20.16).

Steven Chase has a helpful analysis of the implications
of prayer as a conversation with God. The Latin word *colloquium* (conversation)

also means a sharing of words, a discourse, or a simple talk together. The deeper meaning then of
"familiar" conversation connotes acquaintanceship,

intimacy, friendship, and ultimately the safe, shared, and loving conversation one might find within a family. . . . Prayer as conversation with God is the primary speech of the true self to the true God. In prayer, we come to live and dwell in a familiar, intimate, and loving way with God.[51]

In his first catechism (1538) Calvin defines prayer differently, but it encapsulates much of what he has to say in later discussions of prayer in his commentaries and sermons.

Since prayer is a sort of agreement (*arbitri instar*) between us and God whereby we pour out before him all the desires, joys, sighs, and finally, thoughts of our hearts, we must diligently see to it, as often as we call upon the Lord, that we descend into the innermost recesses of our hearts and from that place, not from the throat and tongue, call God.[52]

This more popular notion of pouring out our hearts and souls to God in prayer is found in many places in Calvin's writings. For example, in his commentary on Isaiah 63:16 he states, "God permits us to reveal our hearts familiarly before him; for prayer is nothing else than the opening up of our heart before God." For in prayer we can "pour our cares, distresses and anxieties into his bosom." As David says, "Cast your cares on the Lord" (Ps. 37:5).[53] As long as we restrain ourselves "within due limits," says Calvin, we may "freely pour forth our feelings" in prayer, including our "griefs and anxieties," and "pour them into the bosom of God."[54]

Calvin is fond of this last expression, namely, laying our

concerns on the bosom of God. We "give proof of our faith," he says, "when we turn to God and cast all our cares on his bosom and lay before him all our desires."[55] Christ here is our model. We can learn from his prayer in the Garden of Gethsemane that "where God is the sole judge and there is no fear of self-seeking, there the faithful soul uncovers itself more intimately and in greater simplicity, unburdens its desires, sighs, anxieties, fears, hopes, and joys into the lap of God."[56] In short, "the end of praying is that every one of us pour forth, as it is said in the Psalms, his heart before God."[57]

Why Pray?

This might seem like a strange question in view of all that has been discussed above. However, especially given the fundamental tenets of Calvin's theology, it is not an unreasonable question. That is, if God knows our needs before we ask him, what is the point of prayer? God, after all, knows our needs without being told. Calvin is quite aware of this objection and asks, "But, someone will say, does God not know, even without being reminded, both in what respect we are troubled and what is expedient for us, so that it may seem in a sense superfluous that he should be stirred up by our prayers—as if he were drowsily blinking or even sleeping until he is aroused by our voice?" (*Inst.* 3.20.3). Calvin's response to such an absurd notion is that God "ordained [prayer] not so much for his own sake as for ours" (ibid.). We may be "dull and stupid" in the midst of our problems but while God "keeps guard on our behalf, and sometimes even helps us unasked, still it is very important for us to call upon him . . . [and] in every need to flee to him as to a sacred anchor" (ibid.).

In a sermon on 2 Samuel 7:25–29, Calvin observes that David prays that his house will be "established forever" even though God had assured him earlier that he would do this. It seems, therefore, says Calvin, that this prayer would be "superfluous." "On the contrary," says Calvin, "these things are inseparable," namely,

> the prayer itself and the desire which we have to pray for God to accomplish it all and make us feel it in reality. When, therefore, we pray to God, it is not that we are doubting whether he is already inclined to do us good; or whether he watches out to support us in all our necessities. . . . Rather, the fact is that our faith ought to be exercised, and that God, in offering us his mercy and grace, invites us to have the boldness to call upon him (Eph. 2:18). Without this he cannot give us free access.[58]

This brings to mind two parables of Jesus, which at first glance seem to suggest that God needs to be coerced into answering our prayers. The one is about the so-called "importunate" or persistent widow who kept hounding the hardhearted judge until he relented and offered to help her. Calvin recognizes that the lesson here is persistence in prayer. Moreover, what is not being taught here is that God is "overcome by our prayers and at last unwillingly moved to mercy." Rather, the point is that "God does not help his people immediately because in a sense he wants them to tire themselves out with praying." This is an odd way of putting the matter, but it corresponds to Calvin's constant refrain that one of the purposes of prayer is to *exercise* our faith. In any case, the comparison here between God and the cruel judge "is not completely applicable, for there is a big difference between an ungodly cruel man and the God who inclines to mercy."[59]

In the case of the parable of the man who wants to borrow bread from a friend at midnight (Luke 11:5–13), Calvin's comment is brief and to the point.

> There is no reason for the faithful to grow weary at heart if they do not at once obtain their requests, or if what they ask for seems difficult to achieve, for if you can put pressure on men by importunity in asking, when a man will not do a thing for you willingly, we should have no doubt that God will attend to our prayer if we persist at it with resolution and do not let our hearts faint through delay or difficulty.[60]

Calvin does not discuss either of these parables in his chapter on prayer in the *Institutes*, but in another context and elsewhere he stresses the importance of perseverance in prayer. "Persevere in prayer," he urges, "and, with desires suspended, patiently . . . wait for the Lord. Then we shall be sure that, even though he does not appear, he is always present to us, and will in his own time declare how he has never had ears deaf to the prayers that in men's eyes he seems to have neglected" (*Inst.* 3.20.51). In the Preface to his commentary on the Psalms he writes: "Even when in the midst of doubts, fears, and apprehensions, let us put forth our efforts in prayer, until we experience some consolation which may calm and bring contentment to our minds. Although distrust may shut the gate against our prayers, yet we must not allow ourselves to give way . . . but must persevere until faith finally comes forth victorious from these conflicts."[61]

When the apostle urges us to "continue in prayer,"

Calvin concludes that Paul "commends here two things in prayer: first, assiduity; second, alacrity or earnest intentness."[62] In Romans 12:12—"continue steadfastly in prayer"—Calvin sees another call for perseverance, "because our warfare is unceasing and various assaults arise daily."[63] Therefore, "we must repeat the same supplications not twice or three times only, but as often as we need, a hundred and a thousand times. . . . We must never be weary in waiting for God's help."[64] However, such perseverance is not easy. Calvin, accordingly interprets the phrase in Jude 20—"praying in the Holy Spirit"—to mean that "such is the laziness and coldness of our makeup that none can succeed in praying as he ought without the prompting of the Spirit of God."[65]

The Rules of Right Prayer

The chapter on prayer in the *Institutes* is not so much a theology of prayer as a handbook on how to pray properly. Toward this end Calvin suggests four ways for "framing prayer duly and properly" (*Inst.* 3.20.4). The following is a brief summary since the full text (*Inst.* 3.20.4–14) is found on pp. 53–76 below.

1. The first is "that we be disposed in mind and heart as is suitable for those who enter into conversation with God" (3.20.4). Here Calvin is warning against undisciplined and irreverent prayer. However, he also reminds those who might therefore be timid or afraid that they can rely on the help of the Holy Spirit as promised in Romans 8:26 (3.20.5).

2. "That in our petitions we always have a sense of our own insufficiency, and earnestly pondering how we

need all that we seek, join with this prayer an earnest—nay, burning—desire to attain it" (3.20.6). Prayers that are not offered sincerely and seriously are a mockery to God (ibid.). The presupposition for lawful prayer is a spirit of repentance and a zeal for the Kingdom of God (3.20.7).

3. "That anyone who stands before God to pray, in his humility giving glory completely to God, abandon all thought of his own glory, cast off all notion of his own worth, in short, put away all self-assurance . . ." (3.20.8). . . . We can and should be confident as we approach God in prayer, but this confidence derives solely from God's mercy. Every prayer must be accompanied by a confession of guilt and a plea for pardon (3.20.9).

4. "The fourth rule is that, thus cast down and overcome by true humility, we should nevertheless be encouraged to pray for a sure hope that our prayer will be answered." Confident faith and reverent fear go together (3.20.11; cf. 3.20.14). "Only that prayer is acceptable to God which is born . . . out of such presumption of faith and is grounded in unshaken hope" (3.20.12). But this is possible only for those who know the good news that God in Jesus Christ is "gentle and kind" to all who call upon him in repentance and faith (3.20.14; cf. 3.20.12).[66]

In his other writings Calvin gives further instructions—and admonitions—as to how we should pray and also what is faulty or defective prayer. First, the latter. doubtful prayer, for example, "is no prayer at all," as far as Calvin is concerned.[67] Calvin also constantly urges moderation in our prayers, which is the opposite of praying "with vehemence and impetuosity."[68] We must also beware of making demands of God that are rash, self-centered, unworthy, and not according to the will of God.[69] Even worse, some people try to "dictate terms to the Almighty."[70] According to Calvin, God "abominates" hypocrites who pray to him "deceitfully and dishonestly (Ps. 145:18; Isa. 29:13)."[71] And we insult God if our prayers are "careless and lighthearted."[72]

On the positive side of the ledger, the first step toward appropriate and effective prayer is that it "spring from repentance and faith."[73] We must begin by seeking forgiveness of our sins, for "there is no hope of obtaining any favor from God unless he is reconciled to us."[74] We must humble ourselves before God with a spirit of penitence.[75] At the same time, we must come with confidence, trusting that God will answer our prayers. Calvin spells this out, and more, in his comments on James 1:6: "But let him ask in faith."

> Prayer has its due order and method, and this is his first lesson. We are not able to pray unless the Word leads our way: likewise before we pray, we must believe. Our praying is testimony that we look hopefully to God for the grace he has promised. One who has no faith in the promises is praying in pretence. . . . Faith which relies on the promises of God assures us that we shall receive what we ask for: consequently, it goes with a confidence and a certainty of the love God has for us.[76]

Calvin believes that for the apostle Paul "it is axiomatic that we cannot rightly pray unless we are persuaded for certain of success." Paul is referring here (in Rom. 10:14) "to that certainty which our minds must conceive of God's fatherly kindness, when he reconciles us to himself by the Gospel and adopts us as his children. By this confidence alone we have access to him, as we are also taught in Ephesians 3:12."[77]

In his Geneva Catechism, Calvin refers again to Romans 10:14—a key passage to which he refers frequently when discussing prayer—and comes to a similar conclusion. The minister asks, "When we pray, do we do it fortuitously, uncertain of success, or ought we to hold it for sure and certain that God will hear us?" The child is to answer,

> This is the constant foundation of prayer, that we shall be heard by God, and that we shall obtain whatever we demand, in so far as it is expedient for us. For this reason, Paul teaches that true invocation arises from faith (Rom.10:14). For no one will ever rightly call upon God unless he has a prior and certain trust in his goodness.[78]

This is just the beginning. "We come into God's presence with calm confidence only when we bring with us the testimony of heart conscious of what is right and good."[79] Our prayers must also "proceed from a well-disposed and earnest mind" and should "not only be made with our mouth, but also come from the bottom of our heart."[80] Calvin makes this latter point in a variety of ways. It is appropriate to pray with the tongue, that is, verbally, but not with "artificial eloquence. . . . The best grace we can have before God consists in pure simplicity." There is actually a reciprocal relationship between verbal prayer and that which issues silently from the heart. On the one hand, "the heart ought to move and direct the tongue to prayer; but as it often flags or performs its duty in a slow and sluggish manner, it requires that it be aided by the tongue. . . . As the heart ought to go before the words and frame them, so the tongue aids and remedies the coldness and torpor of the heart."[81]

There is a time and a place for personal spoken prayers, but Calvin is generally more concerned about sincerity of heart. This comes out clearly in a recently discovered fragment of a sermon on Acts 2:46–47.

> We not only must serve God and call on him with only our mouth and voice, but that it is necessary that our heart be lifted up so that our melody rises above the heavens and comes right before the majesty of God.
>
> Now it is true that to attain this, it is not necessary that the tongue labors too much. For they who have spoken not a word have sometimes really called out to God, and he has heard and answered them. . . . He knows what we need before we ask it of him. He thus looks into our heart and gives it more attention than he does to the voice of the mouth. For there are many who cry out enough, but it is nothing more than a voice sounding in the air. All this is of no use unless the heart is touched. For if we desire that God hears us and answers our prayers, it is necessary that the heart speaks and is burning with a strong desire to pray to him and praise him.[82]

Calvin has set the bar so high that few people, if any, will have considered themselves qualified for right or proper prayer. Fortunately, Calvin himself seemed to recognize that God will honor and answer our prayers despite all our faults and failures. He seems to be speaking for himself when he writes, "You will find no one who is unaffected by depression and alarms of the flesh. But ultimately temptations of this sort must be overcome by faith, just as a tree puts down firm roots, and though it is shaken by the beat of the storm is not torn down, and in fact, it holds its ground all the more." This concession follows immediately after the statement that "the Lord only heeds our prayers when we bring to them the confidence that they will be heeded."[83]

Calvin finds further comfort in Jesus' experience in the Garden of Gethsemane. Believers' prayers, he concedes, "do not always flow on a straight course to their ending. They do not always keep an even moderation . . . but rather are involved and confused and even in conflict with themselves, or stopping in midstream, just as a ship tossed by storms makes for any harbor, and cannot hold to its right and regular course in a quiet sea."[84]

Such confessions are not unusual. Although Calvin greatly admires Daniel's prayer life, he finds that even Daniel "wrestles with distrust" (in 9:17), but quickly adds that this "was not for his own sake privately, but for that of the whole church to whom he set forth the true method of prayer."

> And experience teaches all the godly how necessary this remedy is in those doubts which break into all our prayers, and make our earnestness and ardor in prayer grow dull and cold within us, or at least we pray without any composed or tranquil confidence, and their trembling vitiates whatever we had formerly conceived.[85]

This is a remarkable concession, but the answer to what appear to be conflicting claims about prayer lies in God's grace in accepting flawed prayers. Even though saints may "aim at the right mark," they "often stumble and fall . . . even in their prayers." Thus all our prayers "would be vitiated if the Lord in his boundless indulgence did not pardon them, wiping away all their stains and receive them as if they were pure."[86]

Calvin elaborates on this theme in sections 15 and 16 of his chapter on prayer in the *Institutes*. Here he cites a number of cases where biblical characters did not pray as they ought (at least according to Calvin's criteria) and yet God in his mercy hears and answers their prayers. In Psalm 107:6, 13, 19, he finds "prayers which do not reach heaven by faith still are not without effect," thanks to God's graciousness (3.20.15). "God tolerates even our stammering and pardons our ignorance whenever something inadvertently escapes us; as indeed without this mercy there would be no freedom to pray" (3.20.16).

Thus, despite Calvin's high standards and many qualifications for right prayer, this does not mean that Calvin believes that God listens and responds only to prayers of "pure intention, which theologically and psychologically would account for precious few prayers. Calvin recognizes our fallen nature and yet exhibits his overriding pastoral compassion, noting that God 'harkens to perverted prayer' as well"[87] (in *Inst.* 3.20.15).

The Lord's Prayer[88]

The best way to pray properly is to follow the example of the prayer our Lord himself taught us. God in his mercy gives us this model prayer as a guide.[89] In this prayer we are requesting "nothing unacceptable to [Christ]—since we are asking almost in his own words."[90] In its six brief petitions is "comprehended everything that is legitimate and expedient for us to pray for."[91] As Calvin understands the prayer, the first three petitions are concerned with the glory of God alone; the latter three are concerned with our welfare and what is useful for us. However, even that which glorifies God works to our benefit, and in the latter three petitions we in turn must keep in view the glory of God.[92]

Because there is a full exposition of the Lord's Prayer in the *Institutes* 3.20.34–47 and since some of the topics discussed there have already been dealt with, I will only focus on four motifs. First, everything that Calvin says about the prayer revolves around the reconciling work of Jesus Christ. We pray in or through the name of Jesus because he is the only mediator between God and humankind (see 1 Tim. 2:5–6). Therefore, every time we pray, we can do so with the assurance that we have a friend in the presence of the heavenly Father "by whose intercession the Father is for us rendered gracious and easily entreated" (3.20.19).

Thereby our relationship to God as Father is such that we can be freed from fear and apprehension when we dare to address him as "our *Father* in heaven." "By the great sweetness of this name [God] frees us from all distrust, since no greater feeling of love can be found elsewhere than in the Father." The counterpart is that God's "boundless love toward us" is seen in "the fact that we are called 'children of God' [1 John 3:1]" (3.20.36).[93] The privilege of being able to cry, "Abba, Father" (Gal. 4:6; Rom. 8:15) is granted us not only because of Christ's role as mediator but also because God "gives the Spirit as witness to us of the same adoption" (3.20.37).

The second point worthy of special attention is the corporate nature of the Lord's Prayer. Calvin makes much of the fact that we do not pray to *my* Father but to *our* Father. "From this fact we are warned how great a feeling of brotherly love ought to be among us, since by the same right of mercy and free liberality we are equally children of such a father" (3.20.38). The ethical implications of this application are further spelled out in his catechism. We may all claim God as our own Father, says Calvin, but our Lord used this expression "to accustom us to exercise charity in prayer, not neglecting others in caring only for ourselves."[94] What is remarkable is that on the basis of our calling God "Our Father," Calvin concludes that this should motivate us to "embrace all who are [our] brothers in Christ, not only those whom [we] at present see and recognize as such but all men who dwell on earth" (3.20.38).[95]

The third point has to do with the nature of the kingdom. In his exposition of the second petition, "Thy kingdom come," Calvin originally tended to stress God's reign within the lives of believers and the church. This is particularly the case in his first catechism. There he defines the kingdom in this way: "By his Holy Spirit to act and to rule *over his own people* in order to make the riches of his goodness and mercy conspicuous in all their works" (emphasis mine). This is a rather restricted view, but shortly thereafter he adds, "At the same time we pray that he will cause his light and truth to shine with ever new increases, by which to dispel, snuff out, and destroy the darkness and falsehoods of Satan and his kingdom."[96] In the final edition of the *Institutes*, Calvin defines the kingdom a little differently. "God reigns where men, both by denial of themselves and by contempt of the world and of earthly life, pledge themselves to his righteousness in order to aspire to a heavenly life" (3.20.42). Again, the focus is on personal godliness and on "the zeal for daily progress" in the faith. Also, it seems to be limited to the growth of the church ("that [God] spread and increase them in number"), although the fullness of the kingdom "is delayed to the final coming of Christ when, as Paul teaches, 'God will be all in all' [1 Cor. 15:28]" (ibid.).

In his commentary on the Lord's Prayer, Calvin takes a different tack and emphasizes not only the role of the Spirit in bringing about God's kingdom (as in the *Institutes*) but the role of the Word and the Spirit in the realization of the kingdom. In this prayer, says Calvin, God realizes his reign "partly [as] the effect of the word of preaching, partly of the hidden power of the Spirit."

> He would govern men by his Word, but as the voice alone, without the inward influence of the Spirit, does not reach down into the heart, the two must be brought together for the establishment of God's Kingdom. So we pray that God will show His power both in Word and in Spirit, that the whole world may willingly come over to Him. . . . So the sum of this supplication is that God will illuminate the heart by the light of His Word, bring our hearts to obey His righteousness by the breathing of His Spirit, and restore to order at His will, all that is lying waste upon the face of the earth.[97]

In his commentary, Calvin also makes clear what was only implied before, namely, that God reigns in two ways: in the renewal of the lives of believers and in the overcoming of Satan and all God's enemies. The goal in both cases is to restore order in a confused and disordered world, for disorder and confusion are "the opposite of the kingdom of God."[98]

The fourth matter of special interest is Calvin's interpretation of the petition, "Give us today our daily bread." There is a tradition of interpreting this petition spiritually. Accordingly to Erasmus, for example, the "bread" for which we pray is not mere earthly food. In his *Paraphrases*, Erasmus calls the bread "heavenly doctrine." And for the early Luther "the principal meaning of 'daily bread' is the preaching of the Word."[99] Not so Calvin. He does not hesitate to emphasize the literal, material meaning of the phrase. What is particularly interesting are the wider ramifications of this petition that he sees implied there. After criticizing Erasmus's "supersubstantial" interpretation of bread, which Calvin judges to be "both trifling and contrary to religion," he offers his own view: "Ultimately, this is the real test of our faith, that we look to God for everything, recognize him as the unique source of all benefits, and find the tokens of his fatherly goodness appearing even in the smallest matters, so that he will not refuse to consider the needs of the flesh also."[100]

Thus, for Calvin, "daily bread" implies not only the physical needs of our bodies but also points to God's gracious care for us in all our activities and our need to trust God's providence. By praying this phrase in faith,

> We give ourselves over to God's care, and entrust ourselves to his providence, that he may feed, nourish, and preserve us. For our most gracious Father does not disdain to take even our bodies under his safekeeping and guardianship in order to exercise our faith in these matters, while we expect everything

from him, even to a crumb of bread and a drop of water (*Inst.* 3.20.44).[101]

Trusting in God's providence, however, is no excuse for indolence. At the same time we pray for God to supply our daily needs, we must also do our part. Nevertheless, our labor will be in vain if God does not bless it. "Although we are to work and even sweat to provide food, nevertheless we are not nourished by our labor or industry or diligence, but by God's blessing only, by which the labor of our hands is prospered, which would otherwise be in vain." Moreover the real nourishment we receive from food comes not so much from the substance of the food but from God's goodness and grace.[102] For it is by "[God's] power alone that life and strength are sustained, even though he administers it to us by physical means" (*Inst.* 3.20.44).

Calvin also sees here several ethical dimensions. In passing he warns against greed—wanting more than we need—urges us to be generous as God has been generous to us, and speaks to the situation of the rich who may think this petition is unnecessary for them. "These words tell us," says Calvin, "that unless God feeds us, no amount of accrued capital will mean anything."

> Although grain, wine, and everything else be there to overflowing, if they do not have the dew of God's unseen benediction, these all vanish on the spot, or that enjoyment is taken away, or the power they have to nourish us is lost, and we starve in the midst of great supply. So there is no wonder that Christ invites the rich and poor alike to the heavenly store.[103]

Conclusion

Calvin begins his chapter on prayer with an oft-cited analogy, and with that I would like to close. It serves as a delightful entrance to this famous chapter on prayer, the riches of which have barely been tapped in this introductory essay. He likens "the riches which are laid up for us with the heavenly Father" to treasures that are buried in the ground. To fail to take advantage of the heavenly Father's invitation to pray to him is like a man neglecting "a treasure, buried and hidden in the earth, after it had been pointed out to him" (*Inst.* 3.20.1). The inference is that it would be the height of stupidity not to take advantage of this wonderful possibility. Therefore, we should "dig up by prayer the treasures that were pointed out by the Lord's gospel, and which our faith has gazed upon" (3.20.2). In other words, "So the prayers that we offer are, as it were, keys by which to come to the treasures God reserves for us and which he will not keep from us. Therefore, we must open the way to them by praying."[104]

Notes

1. *Calvin: Institutes of the Christian Religion*, 3.20.1; ed. John T. McNeill, trans. Ford Lewis Battles, 2 vols. Library of Christian Classics (Philadelphia: Westminster Press, 1960), 2:850 n. 1.
2. In English the fullest treatment is by Ronald Wallace, *Calvin's Doctrine of the Christian Life* (Edinburgh: Oliver & Boyd, 1959).
3. Cited in Raymond K. Anderson, "The Principal Practice of Faith," *Christian History* 5, no. 4, 21.
4. T. H. L. Parker, *Calvin: An Introduction to His Thought* (Louisville, KY: Westminster John Knox Press, 1995), 107. However, Parker does qualify this remark later. "Yet prayer is not simply a seeking of God's blessings. Rather, it is a calling, for the presence of his providence caring for us, of his power upholding us and of his goodness receiving us, who are laden with sin, into his favour," 107–8.

5. Ronald Wallace, *Calvin, Geneva, and the Reformation* (Grand Rapids: Wm. B. Eerdmans Publishing Co., 1988), 214.

6. Generally I will be using the McNeill-Battles edition of the *Institutes*. Henceforth, because of the frequent references to the *Institutes*, I shall incorporate references to it in an abbreviated form in the text.

7. This phrase is a part of the title of chapter 20, which reads, "Prayer, Which Is the Chief Exercise of Faith, and by Which We Daily Receive God's Benefits." Calvin repeats this in his commentary on Jeremiah 31:7 (reprint of Edinburgh edition). An interesting contrast is found in the Heidelberg Catechism, Q. 116, which calls prayer "the chief part of gratitude," *The Heidelberg Catechism*, 400th Anniversary Edition, trans. Allen O. Miller and M. Eugene Osterhaven (Boston: United Church Press, 1963).

8. Sermon on 2 Samuel 7:25–29, in *Sermons on 2 Samuel*, chap. 1–13, trans. Douglas Kelly (Carlisle, PA: Banner of Truth Trust, 1992), 392.

9. One who wishes to compare the first and last editions may find an English translation of the former by Ford Lewis Battles: *John Calvin's Institutes of the Christian Religion, 1536 Edition* (Grand Rapids: Wm. B. Eerdmans Publishing Co., 1975). Calvin's Catechism of 1538 is found in *Calvin's First Catechism: A Commentary*, by I. John Hesselink, Battles trans. of the Catechism (Louisville, KY: Westminster John Knox Press, 1997).

10. Elsie Anne McKee, "John Calvin's Teaching on the Lord's Prayer," in *The Lord's Prayer: Perspectives for Reclaiming Christian Prayer*, ed. Daniel L. Migliore (Grand Rapids: Wm. B. Eerdmans Publishing Co., 1993), 88–106.

11. Ibid., 92.

12. Cf. "We are commanded to pray with a sure faith, and the promise is added that whatever we ask believing, it will be given us (Matt. 21:22; Mark 11:24)." *Catechism of the Church of Geneva*, trans. J. K. S. Reid of the 1545 (Latin) edition, Q. 249 (Philadelphia: Westminster Press, 1954), 123.

13. Sermon on 1 Timothy 2:8, in *Grace and Its Fruits. Selections from John Calvin on the Pastoral Epistles*, ed. Joseph Hill (Auburn, MA: Evangelical Press, 2000), 259–60.

14. Sermon on 2 Samuel 7:25–29, trans. Douglas Kelly in *Sermons on 2 Samuel*, 392.

15. Ibid., 393–94.

16. See further Hesselink, *Calvin's First Catechism*, 116–17.

17. Comm. Daniel 10:20, 262. Quotations from the Old Testament commentaries are generally from the Calvin Translation Society edition reprinted by Wm. B. Eerdmans Publishing Co., 1940–50.

18. Geneva Catechism (1545), Q. 248, 121.

19. Comm. on Exodus 29:38, *The Four Last Books of Moses*, vol. 2, 295.

20. Sermon on Genesis 26:23–25 in *Sermons on Election and Reprobation*, trans. John Field (Audubon, NJ: Old Paths Publications, 1996), 210.

21. Geneva Catechism, Q. 252, translation based on the French version by T. F. Torrance in *The School of Faith* (London: James Clarke, 1959), 44. Karl Barth found this a striking utterance and commented, "Calvin even says that we pray through the mouth of Jesus Christ, who speaks for us because of what he has been, because of what he has suffered in obedience and faithfulness to the Father. And we ourselves pray as though with his mouth, inasmuch as he gives us access and audience, and intercedes for us." *Prayer*, 50th Anniversary Edition (Louisville, KY: Westminster John Knox Press, 2002), 14.

22. Comm. John 16:26, 130. All quotations from the New Testament commentaries are from the version edited by David W. Torrance and Thomas F. Torrance (Grand Rapids: Wm. B. Eerdmans Publishing Co., 1959–72).

23. Comm. Genesis 19:18.

24. Comm. Numbers 14:17, *The Last Four Books of Moses*, vol. 4, 75.

25. Comm. Zechariah 13:9, *Minor Prophets*, vol. 5, 403.

26. Comm. James 1:6, 264.

27. Comm. Zechariah 7:1–3, *Minor Prophets*, vol. 5, 167.

28. Sermon on Isaiah 53:12, in *Sermons on Isaiah's Prophecy of the Death and Passion of Jesus Christ*, trans. by T. H. L. Parker (London: James Clarke, 1956), 150.

29. Preface to the Commentary on the Psalms, xxxvii.

30. Ibid., xl, xxxvii. Cf. Barbara Pitkin, "Imitation of David: David as a Paradigm for Faith in Calvin's Exegesis of the Psalms," in *The Sixteenth Century Journal* xxiv, 4 (Winter 1993): 843ff.; and James A. De Jong, "An Anatomy of All Parts of the Soul," "Insights into Calvin's Spirituality from His Psalms Commentary," in *Calvinus Sacrae Scripturae Professor*, ed. Wilhelm Neuser (Grand Rapids: Wm. B. Eerdmans Publishing Co., 1994), 1–14.

31. On the origins of this expression, see Hesselink, *Calvin's First Catechism*, Appendix, 177.

32. Comm. Romans 8:26, 177–78.
33. Comm. Micah 3:4, *Minor Prophets*, vol. 3, 221. Here Calvin speaks of praying with the *heart*. Elsewhere, he says that in prayer the Spirit quickens us so that "the *heart* is truly touched and the understanding, enlightened," Epistle to the Reader, Commentary on Psalms, 1543 version; cited in Elsie McKee, *John Calvin: Writings on Pastoral Piety* (New York: Paulist Press, 2001), 92. McKee provides a chapter of Calvin's prayers in this fine work. There are examples of different kinds of prayers, from the 1542/45 Catechism (with interesting variants) and liturgy, as well as from Calvin's sermons and lectures. Throughout McKee's book there are also various liturgical prayers in their proper liturgical contexts (under Sunday and weekday worship, as well as the prayers of the sacraments in a liturgical setting).
34. Geneva Catechism, Q. 245, Reid trans., 131.
35. Comm. Romans 8:15, 170.
36. Comm. James 1:6, 264–65.
37. There is an interesting variation in Calvin's commentary on Ephesians 6:18: "To call upon God is the chief exercise of faith *and hope*" (emphasis mine), 221.
38. Sermon on 2 Samuel 7:29, 392.
39. Comm. Acts 8:22, 241. Literally, faith is the "mother (*mater*) of prayer."
40. Comm. Zephaniah 3:7, *Minor Prophets*, vol. 4, 284.
41. Comm. Daniel 9:23, 194.
42. Sermon on 1 Timothy 1:1–2 in *Sermons of M. John Calvin, on the Epistles of S. Paule to Timothie and Titus*, trans. L. T. (London: G. Bishop & T. Woodcobe, 1579), 135.
43. Comm. Psalm 119; 58, 443.
44. Comm. Psalm 145; 18, 281.
45. Comm. Habakkuk 3:1, *Minor Prophets*, vol. 4, 133.
46. Comm. Jeremiah 36:7, 333. Prior to this comment Calvin says, "In prayer two things are necessary—faith and humility: by faith we rise up to God, and by humility we lie prostrate on the ground," 332.
47. Jesus (in Matt. 17:19–21) "prescribes prayer" as "the remedy for languid faith." Therefore, "faith must be stirred up by prayers," Comm. Matthew 17:19–21, 210.
48. Sermon on Ephesians 6:18, 677.
49. Calvin elaborates this point about prayer and providence with a

colorful expression: God, he says, "ever extends his hand to help his own, not wet-nursing them with words (*nec lactare eos verbis*) but defending them with present help" (3.20.3).

50. 3.20.5, 16. Earlier in section 4, Calvin describes prayer simply as a "conversation" and uses a Latin variant, viz., *colloquium*. A note in the McNeill-Battles edition of the *Institutes* points out that several church fathers used the same word to describe prayer, e.g., Augustine, Benedict, and Aquinas, 853. They might also have mentioned Clement of Alexandria in *Stromata* VII: "Prayer is conversation with God." John Allen also translates *colloquium* as "conversation," but translates *familiare alloquium* as "familiar intercourse" (translation of the *Institutes* in 1813, Eerdmans reprint 1949). In a sermon on Eph. 6:18–19, Calvin refers to prayer as "a mutual communication," 689.

51. Steven Chase, *The Tree of Life: Models of Christian Prayer* (Grand Rapids: Baker Academic, 2005), 59. In a note, Chase adds, "Openness and trust implied in the image of prayer as 'familiar conversation' is prayer focused not only on self, neighbor, and world, but also on God," 262, n. 6. Chase follows his discussion of Calvin in this context with the example of the French Carmelite, Brother Lawrence, who also thought of prayer as primarily conversation with God, 59ff.

52. This is found in Hesselink, *Calvin's First Catechism*, 28. Calvin is not averse to verbal prayers, as we shall see later. The point is that what we say with the tongue must reflect sincerity of heart.

53. Comm. Isaiah 63:16, 353.

54. Comm. Habakkuk 1:2, *Minor Prophets*, vol. 4, 19.

55. Comm. Daniel 6:10, T. H. L. Parker trans. (Grand Rapids: Wm. B. Eerdmans Publishing Co., 1993), 247.

56. Comm. Matthew 26:39, vol. 3, 149. Calvin uses the words *heart* and *soul* almost interchangeably. "For him the soul is the living core of the believer's subjective feelings, attitudes, responses, and convictions." It does not mean simply "life" since this meaning is "very cold and unsatisfactory." As he says of Psalm 34:2, "The term 'soul' . . . signifies not the vital spirit but the seat of the affections," cited in De Jong, "An Anatomy of All Parts of the Soul," in *Calvinus Sacrae Scripturae Professor*, ed. Neuser, 5.

57. Comm. Habakkuk 1:2, 19.

58. *Sermons on 2 Samuel*, Kelly trans., 387.

59. Comm. Luke 18:1–7, vol. 2, 125.

60. Comm. Luke 11:5, vol. 2, 231.
61. Comm. Psalms, xxxviii.
62. Comm. Colossians 4:2, 356.
63. Comm. Romans 12:12, 273.
64. Sermon on Ephesians 47:18–19, 683.
65. Comm. Jude 20, 334.
66. This summary is taken verbatim from Hesselink, *Calvin's First Catechism*, 131–32.
67. Comm. Psalm 140:12, vol. 5, 232.
68. Comm. Joshua 7:6, 107.
69. Comm. Psalm 58:6, vol. 2, 374; Comm. Daniel 6:10, Parker trans., 250.
70. Comm. Psalm 55:22, vol. 2, 344.
71. Geneva Catechism (1545), Q. 241.
72. Comm. Psalm 102:1, vol. 2, 97. In his sermon on Ephesians 6:18, Calvin similarly disparages hypocrisy, mumbling our prayers, and praying for "selfish and frivolous things," 679.
73. Comm. Daniel 9:13, vol. 2, 170.
74. Comm. Psalm 25:7, vol. 1, 419.
75. Comm. Daniel 10:12, vol. 2, 249–50.
76. Comm. James 1:6, 264–65.
77. Comm. Romans 10:14, 230.
78. Geneva Catechism (1545), Q. 248.
79. Comm. 1 John 3:21, 279. "None can really call upon God save those who fear and worship him aright with a pure heart," Comm. 1 John 3:22, 280.
80. Sermon on Ephesians 6:18, 679.
81. Comm. Psalm 102:1, vol. 4, 97–98.
82. "A Fragment from a Sermon of John Calvin," ed. and trans. Erik A. de Boer, *Calvin Theological Journal* 34/1 (April 1999): 178. We must also "lift up our hearts in such a way that we may be in the presence of God," Sermon on Ephesians 6:18, 682.
83. Comm. James 1:6, 265.
84. Comm. Matthew 21:21, vol. 3, 149.
85. Comm. Daniel 9:17, vol. 2, 179.
86. Comm. Joshua 7:6, 107.
87. Chase, *The Tree of Life*, 262, n. 4.
88. For a critical analysis of Calvin's treatment of the Lord's Prayer, tracing its development in Calvin's writings, see McKee, "John Calvin's Teaching on the Lord's Prayer," in *The Lord's Prayer*, ed. Daniel Migliore.

89. McKee, "The Lord's Prayer is our perfect model, but this does not mean that we are constrained to use only its precise words. Calvin himself did not hesitate to paraphrase the text for Sunday worship, to enable the people to understand better what they were asking," ibid., 94.

90. Calvin's First Catechism (1538), 24, in Hesselink, *Calvin's First Catechism*, 29.

91. Geneva Catechism, Q. 255, 122.

92. Ibid., Qs. 258–59, 123.

93. "God assumes this name [Father], which suggests nothing but kindness." Geneva Catechism, Q. 260, 123.

94. Ibid., Q. 263, 124.

95. Jan Milic Lochman sees in these "remarkable words" further evidence of "the social dimensions of prayer," "The Lord's Prayer in Our Time" in *The Lord's Prayer*, ed. Migliore, 15.

96. In Hesselink, *Calvin's First Catechism*, 24.iii, 30. This is almost repeated in the latter part of Q. 269 in the Geneva Catechism. In the first part of the answer concerning what is meant by the phrase "thy kingdom come," the explanation is limited to the "daily increase of the number of the faithful"; but then Calvin adds that the Lord may "render conspicuous and apparent his truth for the dispersal more and more of the darkness of Satan. . . ." 125.

97. Comm. Matthew 6:10, vol. 1, 208.

98. Ibid.

99. McKee, in *The Lord's Prayer*, 100.

100. Comm. Matthew 6:12, vol. 1, 209.

101. In his sermon on Micah 2:1–3, Calvin calls avarice "the root of the evils that reign among mankind." The remedy "lies in trusting in the providence of God, as well as in understanding the intent of the Lord's Prayer: 'Give us this day our daily bread.'" *John Calvin: Sermons on the Book of Micah*, trans. and ed. Benjamin Wirt Farley (Phillipsburg, NJ: P & R Publishing, 2003), 71.

102. Geneva Catechism, Q. 276, 126. Calvin refers here and in the *Institutes* also to Deut. 8:3. Cf. Lev. 26:26 and Ezek. 4:16–17; 14:13.

103. Comm. Matthew 6:12, vol. 1, 210. "The rich, like the poor, should hold this for certain, that nothing they have will profit them, unless in so far as God allows them its use and grants by his grace that its use be fruitful and efficacious." Geneva Catechism, Q. 279, 126.

104. Sermon on Ephesians 6:18, 678.

A Selection of Calvin's Prayers

In addition to discussing Calvin's understanding of prayer and its importance in the Christian life, it may be instructive to examine some of Calvin's prayers. Unfortunately, there is no complete collection of the reformer's prayers, but we do have access to some of his set prayers for special occasions, such as a morning and evening prayer, a prayer before one goes to work, a grace before meals, and the prayers he ordinarily used before and after his sermons.[1]

I. The Formal, Set Prayers

These prayers are longer than the very brief extemporaneous prayers Calvin offered after each of his lectures on the prophets, and differ somewhat in their nature. In the former the following characteristics stand out:

1. *The form of address to God.* It is not so much the sovereignty or majesty of God but rather the father-

hood of God that is prominent. For example, "My God, my Father and preserver"; "O Lord God, most merciful Father and Savior"; or "Let us call upon our good God and Father."[2]

2. *Confession of sin.* Invariably Calvin acknowledges specific sins, even in these generic prayers: indolence, torpor, the cravings of the flesh, greedy affection or desire of gain, distrust (of God), and lack of patience.

3. *An appeal to God's mercy and grace in Jesus Christ.* May it please God "to look upon us in the face of his well-beloved Son our Lord Jesus." "May I look for all happiness only to thy grace and kindness." "Increase the gifts of thy grace to me from day to day, while so much the more I cleave to thy Son Jesus Christ, whom we justly call the true Sun, perpetually shining in our hearts."

4. *A request for God's guidance, particularly that of the Holy Spirit.*[3] "As thou dost illumine this world by the sun . . . , so enlighten my mind by the illumination of thy Spirit and guide me through him in the way of righteousness." "So govern my heart that I may willingly and eagerly set myself to profit. . . . " "May it please God to guide with his Holy Spirit all kings, princes, and magistrates. . . ."

5. *Exhortation to glorify God in all of life.* "May all my actions conduce to the glory of thy name (and the welfare of my brethren)." May we "serve and honor God by glorifying his holy name in all our life. . . ." May God give his faithful ones who are persecuted "such a true steadfastness that his holy name may be glorified by them both in life and death." And in his evening prayer Calvin prays that while sleeping God

will keep him "chaste and pure" and "safe from all perils, so that even my sleep may yield glory to thy name."

II. The Extemporaneous Prayers[4]

The brief prayers that follow Calvin's lectures on the prophets were apparently given extemporaneously. Most of the above themes are found also in these prayers, but they usually reflect the subject of the preceding biblical exposition. More important and especially noteworthy is the way Calvin concludes the vast majority of these prayers, that is, with an eschatological motif—with a view to the consummation of all things and the full coming of the reign of God. For example, these prayers typically end with phrases like "until at length . . . we be gathered into the celestial kingdom," or "that having finished our warfare we may at last enjoy that blessed rest which thou hast promised to us and which is laid up for us in heaven. . . ."[5]

The following four prayers illustrate this point and show how these eschatological endings are integrated into the prayer as a whole.[6]

Almighty God, since you so kindly invite us to yourself and do not cease, even if we are deaf, to extend your grace toward us, grant that we obey you willingly and allow ourselves to be ruled by your Word. And grant that we might obey you steadfastly, not only for a day or a short time, but *until we have completed the course of our journey and are gathered together in your heavenly rest*, through Christ our Lord. Amen.[7]

Almighty God, since you have today made yourself known to us so intimately in the gospel of Christ our Lord, grant that we might learn to lift our eyes to the light set before us, and keep them there fixed, so that we may be directed ever to hold to the path and struggle to reach the goal to which you call us; *until at last, having completed the course of our calling, we attain to you and enjoy with you that glory which your only-begotten Son has won for us by his blood.* Amen.[8]

Almighty God, since you have condescended to approach us so intimately, grant that we in turn may eagerly approach you and abide in firm and holy communion. While we continue in the legitimate worship that you prescribe for us in your Word, may your benefits to us also increase, *until you lead us to their fullness when you gather us together into your heavenly kingdom*, through Jesus Christ, our Lord. Amen.[9]

Almighty God, since we are the work and creation of your hands, grant us to realize that we do not live and move except in you alone. And grant, we pray, that we would be so subject to you that we are not only ruled by your hidden providence but also give such evidence of our willing obedience and submission to you, as children should, that we zealously glorify your name on earth, *until we attain to the enjoyment of that blessed inheritance which is laid up for us in heaven*, through Christ our Lord. Amen.[10]
[emphasis added]

There could hardly be a better illustration of Calvin's conviction that a key component of the Christian life is a

"meditation on the future life."[11] In these expositions
Calvin is very concerned with the issues of daily life, but
as these prayers indicate, the affairs of this world must
always be seen in the light of eternity (*sub specie aeterni-
tatis*).

Notes

1. Most of these prayers are appended to the original version of the
   Geneva Catechism, but are not included in the version found in
   Calvin: Theological Treatises of the Library of Christian Classics.
   They are included, however, in A. Mitchell Hunter's *Teaching of
   Calvin* (London: James Clarke, 2d ed., 1950), 215–21. These and
   a few other prayers are also included in *John Calvin: The Christian
   Life*, ed. John H. Leith (San Francisco: Harper & Row, 1984),
   78–82. Most of these prayers are taken from the larger collection
   in *Calvin's Tracts and Treatises*, vol. 2, trans. and ed. by Henry Bev-
   eridge (Grand Rapids: Wm. B. Eerdmans Publishing Co., 1958).
2. This and the following passages are all taken from the prayers
   found in Hunter, 215–21.
3. On the guidance and leading of the Spirit in Calvin's theology see
   my essay, "Governed and Guided by the Spirit—A Key Issue in
   Calvin's Doctrine of the Holy Spirit," in *Das Reformierte Erbe*, Teil
   2, Festschrift for Gottfried Locher, ed. Heiko Oberman, Ernst
   Saxer, et al. (Zurich: Zwingli Verlag, 1993).
4. A representative selection of these prayers and a brief selection
   from the exposition they follow are found in *Calvin's Devotions and
   Prayers of John Calvin*, compiled by Charles E. Edwards (Grand
   Rapids: Baker Book House, 1954).
5. These two phrases follow respectively the exposition of Amos
   8:11–12 (the 66th lecture on the Minor Prophets) and Obadiah
   1:12–21 (lecture 71).
6. These prayers are all taken from the Rutherford House translation of Calvin's Commentary on Ezekiel, chaps. 1–12, translated
   by D. Foxgrover and D. Martin (Grand Rapids: Wm. B. Eerdmans Publishing Co., 1994). These were to be Calvin's last biblical expositions. In fact, he could not complete them and only got
   through chapter 20. He completed this lecture on February 2,

1564, and then was forced to remain at home, largely confined to his bed. He died May 27, 1564.

7. Comm. on Ezekiel 3:21ff., lecture 11, 110. In contrast to all the formal general prayers, these prayers all begin simply with "Almighty God. . . ."

8. Comm. on Ezekiel 4:5ff., lecture 14, 137.

9. Comm. on Ezekiel 8:15ff., lecture 23, 217.

10. Comm. on Ezekiel 10:6ff., lecture 26, 244.

11. The title of chap. 9 of book 3 of the *Institutes*, which forms the climax of his discourse on the Christian life (chaps. 6–10). The final chapter of this discourse is entitled "How We Must Use the Present Life and Its Helps." What I have called a "discourse" came to be known after the 1550 edition of the *Institutes* as "The Little Book on the Christian Life," and in this form was published separately. It was very popular in an earlier period and is available in English as *Golden Book of the Christian Life* (Grand Rapids: Baker Book House, 1952).

"Prayer, Which Is the Chief Exercise of Faith, and by Which We Daily Receive God's Benefits"
(*Institutes* 3.20)

3.20.1–3 The Nature and Value of Prayer

In these three sections, Calvin discusses the nature and value of prayer as a central feature of the Christian life. Prayer is a necessary part of Christian existence. God is the "bestower of all good things, who invites us to request them of him" (sec. 1). Whatever we need and lack is in God and in Jesus Christ.

To neglect going to God and requesting his goodness is like neglecting a treasure hidden in a field. Prayer is necessary because we are so helpless by ourselves. When we pray, we can "rest fully in the thought that none of our ills is hid from him who, we are convinced, has both the will and the power to take the best care of us" (sec. 2).

There are good reasons for prayer, says Calvin, and while at times God appears to be sleeping or idle, God is really trying to "train us, otherwise idle and lazy, to seek, ask, and entreat him to our great good" (sec. 3).

For Reflection and Discussion

1. Why is prayer a necessity in the Christian life?
2. Do you find Calvin's six reasons to pray persuasive? Why or why not?
3. Have you experienced times when God appears to be asleep or idle? When? Did God eventually answer your prayers?

(The nature and value of prayer, 1–3)
1. Faith and prayer

From those matters so far discussed, we clearly see how destitute and devoid of all good things man is, and how he lacks all aids to salvation. Therefore, if he seeks resources to succor him in his need, he must go outside himself and get them elsewhere. It was afterward explained to us that the Lord willingly and freely reveals himself in his Christ. For in Christ he offers all happiness in place of our misery, all wealth in place of our neediness; in him he opens to us the heavenly treasures that our whole faith may contemplate his beloved Son, our whole expectation depend upon him, and our whole hope cleave to and rest in him. This, indeed, is that secret and hidden philosophy which cannot be wrested from syllogisms. But they whose eyes God has opened surely learn it by heart, that in his light they may see light [Ps. 36:9].

But after we have been instructed by faith to recognize that whatever we need and whatever we lack is in God, and in our Lord Jesus Christ, in whom the Father willed all the fullness of his bounty to abide [cf. Col. 1:19; John 1:16] so that we may all draw from it as from an overflowing spring, it remains for us to seek in him, and in prayers to ask of him, what we have learned to be in him. Otherwise, to know God as the master and bestower of all good things, who invites us to request them of him, and still not go to him and not ask of him—this would be of as little profit as for a man to neglect a treasure, buried and hidden in the earth, after it had been pointed out to him. Accordingly, the apostle, in order to show that true faith cannot be indifferent about calling upon God, has laid down this order: just as faith is born from the gospel, so through it our hearts are trained to call upon God's name

[Rom. 10:14–17]. And this is precisely what he had said a
little before: the Spirit of adoption, who seals the witness
of the gospel in our hearts [Rom. 8:16], raises up our spirits to dare show forth to God their desires, to stir up
unspeakable groanings [Rom. 8:26], and confidently cry,
"Abba! Father!" [Rom. 8:15].

Now we must more fully discuss this last point, since it
was previously only mentioned in passing and, as it were,
cursorily touched upon.

2. The necessity of prayer

It is, therefore, by the benefit of prayer that we reach
those riches which are laid up for us with the Heavenly
Father. For there is a communion of men with God by
which, having entered the heavenly sanctuary, they appeal
to him in person concerning his promises in order to
experience, where necessity so demands, that what they
believed was not vain, although he had promised it in
word alone. Therefore we see that to us nothing is promised to be expected from the Lord, which we are not also
bidden to ask of him in prayers. So true is it that we dig
up by prayer the treasures that were pointed out by the
Lord's gospel, and which our faith has gazed upon.

Words fail to explain how necessary prayer is, and in
how many ways the exercise of prayer is profitable. Surely,
with good reason the Heavenly Father affirms that the
only stronghold of safety is in calling upon his name [cf.
Joel 2:32]. By so doing we invoke the presence both of his
providence, through which he watches over and guards
our affairs, and of his power, through which he sustains us,
weak as we are and well-nigh overcome, and of his goodness, through which he receives us, miserably burdened
with sins, unto grace; and, in short, it is by prayer that we

call him to reveal himself as wholly present to us. Hence comes an extraordinary peace and repose to our consciences. For having disclosed to the Lord the necessity that was pressing upon us, we even rest fully in the thought that none of our ills is hid from him who, we are convinced, has both the will and the power to take the best care of us.

3. Objection: Is prayer not superfluous? Six reasons for it

But, someone will say, does God not know, even without being reminded, both in what respect we are troubled and what is expedient for us, so that it may seem in a sense superfluous that he should be stirred up by our prayers— as if he were drowsily blinking or even sleeping until he is aroused by our voice? But they who thus reason do not observe to what end the Lord instructed his people to pray, for he ordained it not so much for his own sake as for ours. Now he wills—as is right—that his due be rendered to him, in the recognition that everything men desire and account conducive to their own profit comes from him, and in the attestation of this by prayers. But the profit of this sacrifice also, by which he is worshiped, returns to us. Accordingly, the holy fathers, the more confidently they extolled God's benefits among themselves and others, were the more keenly aroused to pray. It will be enough for us to note the single example of Elijah, who, sure of God's purpose, after he has deliberately promised rain to King Ahab, still anxiously prays with his head between his knees, and sends his servant seven times to look [1 Kings 18:42], not because he would discredit his prophecy, but because he knew it was his duty, lest his faith be sleepy or sluggish, to lay his desires before God.

Therefore, even though, while we grow dull and stupid

toward our miseries, he watches and keeps guard on our behalf, and sometimes even helps us unasked, still it is very important for us to call upon him: First, that our hearts may be fired with a zealous and burning desire ever to seek, love, and serve him, while we become accustomed in every need to flee to him as to a sacred anchor. Secondly, that there may enter our hearts no desire and no wish at all of which we should be ashamed to make him a witness, while we learn to set all our wishes before his eyes, and even to pour out our whole hearts. Thirdly, that we be prepared to receive his benefits with true gratitude of heart and thanksgiving, benefits that our prayer reminds us come from his hand [cf. Ps. 145:15–16]. Fourthly, moreover, that, having obtained what we were seeking, and being convinced that he has answered our prayers, we should be led to meditate upon his kindness more ardently. And fifthly, that at the same time we embrace with greater delight those things which we acknowledge to have been obtained by prayers. Finally, that use and experience may, according to the measure of our feebleness, confirm his providence, while we understand not only that he promises never to fail us, and of his own will opens the way to call upon him at the very point of necessity, but also that he ever extends his hand to help his own, not wet-nursing them with words but defending them with present help.

On account of these things, our most merciful Father, although he never either sleeps or idles, still very often gives the impression of one sleeping or idling in order that he may thus train us, otherwise idle and lazy, to seek, ask, and entreat him to our great good.

Therefore they act with excessive foolishness who, to call men's minds away from prayer, babble that God's providence, standing guard over all things, is vainly importuned with our entreaties, inasmuch as the Lord has not, on the contrary, vainly attested that "he is near . . . to all who call upon his name in truth" [Ps. 145:18, cf. Comm. and Vg.]. Quite like this is what others prate: that it is superfluous for them to petition for things that the Lord is gladly ready to bestow, while those very things which flow to us from his voluntary liberality he would have us recognize as granted to our prayers. That memorable saying of the psalm attests this, and to it many similar passages correspond: "For the eyes of the Lord are upon the righteous, and his ears toward their prayers" [1 Peter 3:12; Ps. 34:15; cf. 33:16, Vg.]. This sentence so commends the providence of God—intent of his own accord upon caring for the salvation of the godly—as yet not to omit the exercise of faith, by which men's minds are cleansed of indolence. The eyes of God are therefore watchful to assist the blind in their necessity, but he is willing in turn to hear our groanings that he may the better prove his love toward us. And so both are true: "that the keeper of Israel neither slumbers nor sleeps" [Ps. 121:4, cf. Comm.], and yet that he is inactive, as if forgetting us, when he sees us idle and mute.

3.20.4–16   The Rules of Right Prayer

Prayer for Calvin is "conversation with God." This underlies all else. Prayer is "intimate conversation" with God, and Calvin proposes rules for prayer, not in order to lock us into a certain form for prayer, but to indicate our attitudes and dispositions as we approach God in prayer. The four rules are: (1) a composed mind and heart (secs. 4–5); (2) a sincere sense of our own insufficiency (secs. 6–7); (3) an abandoning of all self-glory, self-assurance, and a reliance on God's mercy and pardon (secs. 8–10); and (4) a sure hope that all our prayers are answered (secs. 11–16). Yet in all our failings on these, God still answers.

Through all our prayers, the Holy Spirit is our "teacher in prayer, to tell us what is right and temper our emotions" (sec. 5). Prayer demands repentance and while prayers "do not depend upon their worthiness," we should be displeased with our sinfulness when we pray (sec. 7). All prayer depends on God's mercy and pardon (sec. 9), and God promises to be gracious to us (sec. 10). Faith enables us to receive God's promises and provides a release from "anxiety" when we "take refuge in God" and do not doubt that God is ready to "extend his helping hand" (sec. 11). This faith can be experienced in our hearts. Prayers emerge from hope (sec. 12). Our prayers are "grounded in God's promises, and depend upon them" (sec. 14).

For Reflection and Discussion

1. Does prayer seem like "conversation with God" to you? Do you practice "listening" to God as well as "speaking" to God?

2. Why is it important that we understand prayer as grounded in God's command and promise? What theological difference does this make?

3. In what ways are our anxieties relieved when we pray?

(The rules of right prayer, 4–16)
First Rule: reverence, 4–5

4. Devout detachment required for conversation with God

Now for framing prayer duly and properly, let this be the first rule: that we be disposed in mind and heart as befits those who enter conversation with God. This we shall indeed attain with respect to the mind if it is freed from carnal cares and thoughts by which it can be called or led away from right and pure contemplation of God, and then not only devotes itself completely to prayer but also, in so far as this is possible, is lifted and carried beyond itself. Now I do not here require the mind to be so detached as never to be pricked or gnawed by vexations, since, on the contrary, great anxiety should kindle in us the desire to pray. Thus we see that God's saintly servants give proof of huge torments, not to say vexations, when they speak of uttering their plaintive cry to the Lord from the deep abyss, and from the very jaws of death [cf. Ps. 130:1]. But I say that we are to rid ourselves of all alien and outside cares, by which the mind, itself a wanderer, is borne about hither and thither, drawn away from heaven, and pressed down to earth. I mean that it ought to be raised above itself that it may not bring into God's sight anything our blind and stupid reason is wont to devise, nor hold itself within the limits of its own vanity, but rise to a purity worthy of God.

5. Against undisciplined and irreverent prayer

These two matters are well worth attention: first, whoever engages in prayer should apply to it his faculties and efforts, and not, as commonly happens, be distracted by wandering thoughts. For nothing is more contrary to reverence for God than the levity that marks an excess of frivolity utterly devoid of awe. In this matter, the harder we find concentration to be, the more strenuously we ought to labor after it. For no one is so intent on praying that he does not feel many irrelevant thoughts stealing upon him, which either break the course of prayer or delay it by some winding bypath. But here let us recall how unworthy it is, when God admits us to intimate conversation, to abuse his great kindness by mixing sacred and profane; but just as if the discourse were between us and an ordinary man, amidst our prayers we neglect him and flit about hither and thither.

Let us therefore realize that the only persons who duly and properly gird themselves to pray are those who are so moved by God's majesty that freed from earthly cares and affections they come to it. And the rite of raising the hands means that men remember they are far removed from God unless they raise their thoughts on high. As it is also said in the psalm: "To thee . . . I have lifted up my soul" [Ps. 25:1; cf. 24:1, Vg.]. And Scripture quite often uses this expression, "to lift up prayer" [e.g., Isa. 37:4], in order that those who wish God to hear them may not settle down "on their lees" [cf. Jer. 48:11; Zeph. 1:12]. In short, the more generously God deals with us, gently summoning us to unburden our cares into his bosom, the less excusable are we if his splendid and incomparable benefit does not outweigh all else with us and draw us to him, so that we apply our minds and efforts zealously to prayer. This cannot happen unless the mind, stoutly wrestling with these hindrances, rises above them.

We have noted another point: not to ask any more than God allows. For even though he bids us pour out our hearts before him [Ps. 62:8; cf. Ps. 145:19], he still does not indiscriminately slacken the reins to stupid and wicked emotions; and while he promises that he will act according to the will of the godly, his gentleness does not go so far that he yields to their willfulness. Yet in both, men commonly sin gravely; for many rashly, shamelessly, and irreverently dare importune God with their improprieties and impudently present before his throne whatever in dreams has struck their fancy. But such great dullness or stupidity grips them that they dare thrust upon God all their vilest desires, which they would be deeply ashamed to acknowledge to men. Certain profane authors made fun of and even detested this effrontery, but the vice itself has always held sway; and hence it came to pass that ambitious men chose Jupiter as their patron; the miserly, Mercury; those greedy for knowledge, Apollo and Minerva; the warlike, Mars; the lecherous, Venus. Even so today, as I have just suggested, men in their prayers grant more license to their unlawful desires than if equals were jestingly to gossip with equals. Yet, God does not allow his gentle dealing to be thus mocked but, claiming his own right, he subjects our wishes to his power and bridles them. For this reason, we must hold fast to John's statement: "This is the confidence we have in him, that if we ask anything according to his will, he hears us" [1 John 5:14].

The Holy Spirit aids right prayer
But because our abilities are far from able to match such perfection, we must seek a remedy to help us. As we must turn keenness of mind toward God, so affection of heart has to follow. Both, indeed, stand far beneath; nay, more truly, they faint and fail, or are carried in the opposite direction. Therefore, in order to minister to this weakness, God gives us the Spirit as our teacher in prayer, to tell us what is right and temper our emotions. For,

"because we do not know how to pray as we ought, the Spirit comes to our help," and "intercedes for us with unspeakable groans" [Rom. 8:26]; not that he actually prays or groans but arouses in us assurance, desires, and sighs, to conceive which our natural powers would scarcely suffice. And Paul, with good reason, calls "unspeakable" these groans which believers give forth under the guidance of the Spirit; for they who are truly trained in prayers are not unmindful that, perplexed by blind anxieties, they are so constrained as scarcely to find out what it is expedient for them to utter. Indeed, when they try to stammer, they are confused and hesitate. Clearly, then, to pray rightly is a rare gift. These things are not said in order that we, favoring our own slothfulness, may give over the function of prayer to the Spirit of God, and vegetate in that carelessness to which we are all too prone. In this strain we hear the impious voices of certain persons, saying that we should drowsily wait until he overtake our preoccupied minds. But rather our intention is that, loathing our inertia and dullness, we should seek such aid of the Spirit. And indeed, Paul, when he enjoins us to pray in the Spirit [1 Cor. 14:15], does not stop urging us to watchfulness. He means that the prompting of the Spirit empowers us so to compose prayers as by no means to hinder or hold back our own effort, since in this matter God's will is to test how effectually faith moves our hearts.

Second Rule: We pray from a sincere sense of want, and with penitence, 6–7

6. The sense of need that excludes all unreality

Let this be the second rule: that in our petitions we ever sense our own insufficiency, and earnestly pondering how

we need all that we seek, join with this prayer an earnest—
nay, burning—desire to attain it. For many perfunctorily
intone prayers after a set form, as if discharging a duty to
God. And although they admit it to be a necessary remedy for their ills, because it would be fatal to lack the help
of God which they are beseeching, still it appears that they
perform this duty from habit, because their hearts are
meanwhile cold, and they do not ponder what they ask.
Indeed, a general and confused feeling of their need leads
them to prayer, but it does not arouse them, as it were in
present reality, to seek the relief of their poverty. Now
what do we account more hateful or even execrable to
God than the fiction of someone asking pardon for his
sins, all the while either thinking he is not a sinner or at
least not thinking he is a sinner? Unquestionably something in which God himself is mocked! Yet, as I have just
said, mankind is so stuffed with such depravity that for the
sake of mere performance men often beseech God for
many things that they are dead sure will, apart from his
kindness, come to them from some other source, or
already lie in their possession.

A fault that seems less serious but is also not tolerable
is that of others who, having been imbued with this one
principle—that God must be appeased by devotions—
mumble prayers without meditation. Now the godly must
particularly beware of presenting themselves before God
to request anything unless they yearn for it with sincere
affection of heart, and at the same time desire to obtain it
from him. Indeed, even though in those things which we
seek only to God's glory we do not seem at first glance to
be providing for our own need, yet it is fitting that they be
sought with no less ardor and eagerness. When, for example, we pray that "his name be sanctified" [Matt. 6:9; Luke

11:2], we should, so to speak, eagerly hunger and thirst after that sanctification.

7. *Is prayer at times dependent on our passing mood?*

If anyone should object that we are not always urged with equal necessity to pray, I admit it. And to our benefit James gives us this distinction: "Is anyone among you sad? Let him pray. Is any cheerful? Let him sing" [James 5:13 p.]. Therefore common sense itself dictates that, because we are too lazy, God pricks us the more sharply, as occasion demands, to pray earnestly. David calls this a "seasonable time" [Ps. 32:6; 31:6, Vg.] because, as he teaches in many other passages [e.g., Ps. 94:19], the more harshly troubles, discomforts, fears, and trials of other sorts press us, the freer is our access to him, as if God were summoning us to himself.

At the same time Paul's statement is no less true, that we must "pray at all times" [Eph. 6:18; 1 Thess. 5:17]. For however much after our heart's desire affairs may prosperously flow and occasion for happiness surround us on all sides, still there is no point of time when our need does not urge us to pray. A certain man has abundant wine and grain. Since he cannot enjoy a single morsel of bread apart from God's continuing favor, his wine cellars and granaries will not hinder him from praying for his daily bread. Now if we should consider how many dangers at every moment threaten, fear itself will teach us that we at no single time may leave off praying.

Still, we can better recognize this fact in spiritual matters. For when should the many sins of which we are conscious allow us nonchalantly to stop praying as suppliants for pardon of our guilt and penalty? When do temptations yield us a truce from hastening after help? Moreover, zeal for the Kingdom of God and his glory ought so to lay hold on us, not intermittently but constantly, that the same opportunity may ever remain ours. It is therefore not in vain that constancy in prayer is enjoined upon us. I am not yet speaking of perseverance, of which mention will be made later; but Scripture, admonishing us to "pray constantly" [1 Thess. 5:17], accuses us of sloth, for we do not realize how much we need this attentiveness and constancy. By this rule, hypocrisy and wily falsehoods toward God are debarred from prayer—indeed, are banished far away! God promises that "he will be near to all who call upon him in truth" [Ps. 145:18, cf. Comm.], and states that those who seek him with all their heart will find him [Jer. 29:13–14]. For this reason, they who delight in their own foulness aspire not at all. Lawful prayer, therefore, demands repentance. Hence arises the commonplace in Scripture that God does not hearken to the wicked [John 9:31], and that their prayers [cf. Prov. 28:9; Isa. 1:15]—just as their sacrifices [cf. Prov. 15:8; 21:27]—are abominable to him. For it is right that they who bar their hearts should find God's ears closed, and that they who by their hardheartedness provoke his severity should not feel him conciliatory. In Isaiah he threatens in this way: "Even though you multiply your prayers, I will not listen; for your hands are full of blood" [Isa. 1:15, cf. Vg.]. Again, in Jeremiah: "I cried out . . . and they refused to listen; . . . they will cry out in return, and I will not listen." [Jer. 11:7, 8, 11.] For he counts it the height of dishonor for wicked men, who all their lives besmirch his sacred name, to boast of his covenant. Consequently, in Isaiah he complains, when the Jews "draw near to him with their lips . . . their hearts are far from him" [Isa. 29:13 p.]. He does not, indeed, restrict this to prayers alone but declares that falsity in any part of his worship is abhorrent to him. That statement of James applies here. "You seek, and do not receive because you ask wrongly to spend it on your passions" [James 4:3]. It is indeed true, as we shall again see a little later, that the prayers poured out by the godly do not depend upon their worthiness; yet John's warning is not superfluous: "We receive from him whatever we ask because we keep his commandments" [1 John 3:22], while a bad conscience closes the door to us. From this it follows that only sincere worshipers of God pray aright and are heard. Let each one, therefore, as he prepares to pray be displeased with his own evil deeds, and (something that cannot happen without repentance) let him take the person and disposition of a beggar.

Third Rule: We yield all confidence in ourselves and humbly plead for pardon, 8–10
8. We come as humble suppliants for mercy

To this let us join a third rule: that anyone who stands before God to pray, in his humility giving glory completely to God, abandon all thought of his own glory, cast off all notion of his own worth, in fine, put away all self-assurance—blest if we claim for ourselves anything, even the least bit, we should become vainly puffed up, and perish at his presence. We have repeated examples of this submission, which levels all haughtiness, in God's servants; each one of whom, the holier he is, the more he is cast down when he presents himself before the Lord. Thus spoke Daniel, whom the Lord himself commended with so great a title: "We do not pour forth our prayers unto thee on the ground of our righteousnesses but on the ground of thy great mercy. O Lord, hear us; O Lord, be kindly unto us. Hear us, and do what we ask . . . for thine own sake . . . because thy name is called upon over thy people, and over thine holy place" [Dan. 9:18–19, cf. Vg.]. Nor does he, by a devious figure of speech, as some men do, mingle with the crowd as one of the people. Rather he confesses his guilt as an individual, and as a suppliant takes refuge in God's pardon, as he eloquently declares: "When I had . . . confessed my sin and the sin of my people" [Dan. 9:20 p.]. David also enjoins this humility by his own example: "Enter not into judgment with thy servant, for no man living is righteous before thee" [Ps. 143:2; cf. Comm. and Ps. 142:2, Vg.]. In such a form, Isaiah prays: "Behold, thou wert wroth, for we sinned. . . . The world is founded upon thy ways, therefore we shall be saved. . . . And all of us have been full of uncleanness, and all our righteousnesses like a filthy rag; we all have faded like a leaf, and our iniquities, like the wind, scatter us. There is no one who calls upon thy name, who bestirs himself to take hold of thee. For thou hast hid thy face from us, and hast made us to melt away in the hand of our iniquities. Yet, O Lord, thou art our Father; we are the clay, thou art our potter and we are the work of thy hand. Be not angry, O Lord, and remember not iniquity forever. Behold now, consider, we are all thy people" [Isa. 64:5–9, cf. Comm.].

Observe that they depend on no assurance whatever but this alone: that, reckoning themselves to be of God, they do not despair that he will take care of them. Likewise, Jeremiah: "Though our iniquities testify against us, act . . . for thy name's sake" [Jer. 14:7]. For some unknown author, whoever he may be, has written these very true and holy words attributed to the prophet Baruch: "The soul that is sorrowful and desolate for the greatness of her evil, bowed down and feeble, . . . the hungry soul, and the eyes that fail give glory . . . to thee, O Lord. It is not for the righteousnesses of the fathers that we pour out our prayers before thee, and beg mercy in thy sight, O Lord our God" [Baruch 2:18–19 p., cf. Vg.]; but because thou art merciful, "be merciful unto us, for we have sinned before thee" [Baruch 3:2].

9. The plea for forgiveness of sins as the most important part of prayer

To sum up: the beginning, and even the preparation, of proper prayer is the plea for pardon with a humble and sincere confession of guilt. Nor should anyone, however holy he may be, hope that he will obtain anything from God until he is freely reconciled to him; nor can God chance to be propitious to any but those whom he has pardoned. Accordingly, it is no wonder if believers open for themselves the door to prayer with this key, as we learn from numerous passages of The Psalms. For David, asking for something else than remission of his sins, says: "Remember not the sins of my youth, and my transgressions; according to thy mercy remember me, for thy goodness' sake, O Lord" [Ps. 25:7]. Again: "See my affliction and my toil, and forgive all my sins." [Ps. 25:18 p.] Also, in this we see that it is not enough for us to call ourselves to account each day for recent sins if we do not remember those sins which might seem to have been long forgotten.

For the same prophet, elsewhere having confessed one grave offense, on this occasion even turns back to his mother's womb, in which he had contracted the infection [Ps. 51:5], not to extenuate the guilt on the ground of corruption of nature but that, in gathering up the sins of his whole life, the more rigorously he condemns himself, the more easily entreated he may find God. But even though the saints do not always beg forgiveness of sins in so many words, if we diligently ponder their prayers that Scripture relates, we shall readily come upon what I speak of: that they have received their intention to pray from God's mercy alone, and thus always have begun with appeasing him. For if anyone should question his own conscience, he would be so far from daring intimately to lay aside his cares before God that, unless he relied upon mercy and pardon, he would tremble at every approach.

There is also another special confession when suppliants ask release from punishments. It is that at the same time they may pray for the pardon of their sins. For it would be absurd to wish the effect to be removed while the cause remained. We must guard against imitating foolish sick folk, who, concerned solely with the treatment of symptoms, neglect the very root of the disease. We must make it our first concern that God be favorable toward us, rather than that he attest his favor by outward signs, because he wills to maintain this order, and it would have been of small profit to us to have him do us good unless our conscience, feeling him wholly appeased, rendered him altogether lovely [Cant. 5:16]. Christ's reply also reminds us of this; for after he had decided to heal the paralytic, "Your sins," he said, "are forgiven you" [Matt. 9:2]. He thus arouses our minds to that which we ought especially to desire: that God may receive us into grace; then, that in aiding us he may set forth the fruit of reconciliation.

But besides that special confession of present guilt, with which believers plead for the remission of every sin and penalty, the general preface that gains favor for prayers must never be passed over, for unless they are founded in free mercy, prayers never reach God. John's statement can be applied to this: "If we confess our sins, he is faithful and just to forgive . . . , and cleanse us from all unrighteousness" [1 John 1:9, Vg.]. For this reason, under the law prayers had to be consecrated with blood atonement [cf. Gen. 12:8; 26:25; 33:20; 1 Sam. 7:9] in order that they should be accepted, and that the people should thus be warned that they were unworthy of so great a privilege of honor until, purged of their defilement, they derived confidence in prayer solely from God's mercy.

10. Reference to one's own righteousness?

Now the saints sometimes seem to shout approval of their own righteousness in calling upon God for help. For example, David says: "Keep my life, for I am good" [Ps. 86:2 p.]; and similarly, Hezekiah: "Remember . . . O Lord, I beseech thee, how I have walked before thee in truth . . . and have done what is good in thy sight" [2 Kings 20:3 p.; cf. Isa. 38:3]. By such expressions they mean nothing else but that by their regeneration itself they are attested as servants and children of God to whom he promises that he will be gracious. He teaches through the prophet, as we have already seen, that his eyes "are upon the righteous, his ears toward their prayers" [Ps. 34:15; cf. 33:16, Vg.]. Again, through the apostle John: "We shall receive . . . whatever we ask if we keep his commandments" [1 John 3:22 p.]. In these statements he does not set the value of prayer according to the merits of works, but he is pleased to establish the assurance of those who are duly aware of guileless uprightness and innocence, as all believers ought to be. Indeed, what the blind man whose sight was restored says in John's gospel—that God does not listen to sinners [John 9:31]—has been drawn from the very truth of God, provided we understand "sinners" in the customary usage of Scripture, as all persons who slumber and repose in their own sins without any desire for righteousness. For no heart can ever break into sincere calling upon God that does not at the same time aspire to godliness. To such promises, then, correspond the saints' attestations, in which they mention their purity or innocence in order that they may feel, what all God's servants should hope for, made manifest to themselves.

Again, while they are before the Lord comparing themselves with their enemies, from whose iniquity they long to be delivered by his hand, they are commonly found using this sort of prayer. Now it is no wonder if in this comparison they put forward their own righteousness and simplicity of heart in order that, from the equity of the cause itself, they might the more move the Lord to provide them with assistance. The godly man enjoys a pure conscience before the Lord, thus confirming himself in the promises with which the Lord comforts and supports his true worshipers. It is not our intent to snatch this blessing from his breast; rather, we would assert that his assurance his prayers will be answered rests solely upon God's clemency, apart from all consideration of personal merit.

Fourth rule: We pray with confident hope, 11–14
11. Hope and faith overcome fear
The fourth rule is that, thus cast down and overcome by true humility, we should be nonetheless encouraged to pray by a sure hope that our prayer will be answered. These are indeed things apparently contrary: to join the firm assurance of God's favor to a sense of his just vengeance; yet, on the ground that God's goodness alone

raises up those oppressed by their own evil deeds, they very well agree together. For, in accordance with our previous teaching that repentance and faith are companions joined together by an indissoluble bond, although one of these terrifies us while the other gladdens us, so also these two ought to be present together in prayers. And David briefly expresses this agreement when he says: "I through the abundance of thy goodness will enter thy house, I will worship toward the temple of thy holiness with fear" [Ps. 5:7]. Under God's goodness he includes faith, meantime not excluding fear. For not only does his majesty constrain us to reverence but through our own unworthiness, forgetting all pride and self-confidence, we are held in fear.

But "assurance" I do not understand to mean that which soothes our mind with sweet and perfect repose, releasing it from every anxiety. For to repose so peacefully is the part of those who, when all affairs are flowing to their liking, are touched by no care, burn with no desire, toss with no fear. But for the saints the occasion that best stimulates them to call upon God is when, distressed by their own need, they are troubled by the greatest unrest, and are almost driven out of their senses, until faith opportunely comes to their relief. For among such tribulations God's goodness so shines upon them that even when they groan with weariness under the weight of present ills, and also are troubled and tormented by the fear of greater ones, yet, relying upon his goodness, they are relieved of the difficulty of bearing them, and are solaced and hope for escape and deliverance. It is fitting therefore that the godly man's prayer arise from these two emotions, that it also contain and represent both. That is, that he groan under present ills and anxiously fear those to come, yet at the same time take refuge in God, not at all doubting he is ready to extend his helping hand. It is amazing how much our lack of trust provokes God if we request of him a boon that we do not expect.

Prayer and faith

Therefore nothing is more in harmony with the nature of prayers than that this rule be laid down and established for them: that they not break forth by chance but follow faith as guide. Christ calls this principle to the attention of all of us with this saying: "I say unto you, whatever you seek . . . , believe that you will receive it, and it will come to you" [Mark 11:24 p.]. He confirms the same statement in another place: "Whatever you ask in prayer, believing . . . ," etc. [Matt. 21:22]. James is in accord with this: "If any of you lack wisdom, let him ask God, who gives to all men simply and without reproaching. . . . Let him ask in faith, with no wavering" [James 1:5–6 p.]. There, opposing faith to wavering, he most appropriately expresses the force of faith. Nonetheless, what he adds must also be noted: that they who in doubt and perplexity call upon God, uncertain in their minds whether they will be heard or not, will gain nothing [cf. James 1:7]. He even compares these persons to waves that are driven and tossed hither and thither by the wind [James 1:6]. Hence, in another passage, James calls what is right and proper "the prayer of faith" [James 5:15]. Then, since God so often affirms that he will give to each one according to his faith [Matt. 8:13; 9:29; Mark 11:24], he implies that we can obtain nothing apart from faith.

To sum up, it is faith that obtains whatever is granted to prayer. Such is the meaning of Paul's famous statement, which the unwise too little regard: "How will anyone call upon him in whom he has not believed? And who will believe unless he has heard?" [Rom. 10:14 p.]. "Faith comes by hearing, and hearing from the Word of God." [Rom. 10:17.] For, deducing step by step the beginning of prayer from faith, he plainly asserts that God cannot be sincerely called upon by others than those to whom, through the preaching of the gospel, his kindness and gentle dealing have become known—indeed, have been intimately revealed.

12. Against the denial of certainty that prayer is granted

Our opponents do not at all ponder this requirement. Therefore, when we enjoin believers to be convinced with firm assurance of mind that God is favorable and benevolent to them, they think we are saying the most absurd thing of all. Still, if they made any use of true prayer, they would really understand that without that firm sense of the divine benevolence God could not be rightly called upon. Since no one can well perceive the power of faith unless he feels it by experience in his heart, what point is there in arguing with men of this stripe, who clearly show that they have never had anything but an empty imagination? For the value and need of that assurance, which we require, is chiefly learned from calling upon him. He who does not see this shows that he has a very insensate conscience. Let us, then, pass over this class of blind persons, and cleave firmly to the statement of Paul's: God cannot be called upon by any except those who have learned of his mercy from the gospel [Rom. 10:14], and have surely been persuaded that it has been prepared for them.

Now what sort of prayer will this be? "O Lord, I am in doubt whether thou willest to hear me, but because I am pressed by anxiety, I flee to thee, that, if I am worthy, thou mayest help me." This is not the way of all the saints whose prayers we read in Scripture. And the Holy Spirit did not so instruct us through the apostle, who enjoins us to "draw near to the heavenly throne . . . with confidence, that we may receive . . . grace" [Heb. 4:16 p.]; and when he teaches elsewhere that we have boldness and access in confidence through faith in Christ [Eph. 3:12]. If we would pray fruitfully, we ought therefore to grasp with both hands this assurance of obtaining what we ask, which the Lord enjoins with his own voice, and all the saints teach by their example. For only that prayer is acceptable to God which is born, if I may so express it, out of such presumption of faith, and is grounded in unshaken assurance of hope. He could have been content with the simple mention of faith, yet he not only added confidence but also fortified it with freedom or boldness, that by this mark he might distinguish from us the unbelievers, who indeed indiscriminately mingle with us in our prayers to God, but by chance. The whole church prays in this way in the psalm: "Let thy mercy be upon us, even as we have hoped in thee" [Ps. 33:22, Comm.]. Elsewhere the prophet lays down the same condition: "In the day when I call, this I know, that God is with me" [Ps. 56:9, Comm.]. Likewise: "In the morning I will make ready for thee, and watch." [Ps. 5:3, see Comm.] From these words we conclude that prayers are vainly cast upon the air unless hope be added, from which we quietly watch for God as from a watchtower. Paul's order of exhortation agrees with these: for before he urges believers "to pray at all times in the Spirit" with watchfulness and perseverance [Eph. 6:18], he bids them first take up "the shield of faith, . . . the helmet of salvation, and the sword of the Spirit, which is the word of God" [Eph. 6:16–17].

Here let my readers recall what I said before: that faith

is not at all overthrown when it is joined with the acknowledgment of our misery, destitution, and uncleanness. For however much believers may feel pressed down or troubled by a heavy weight of sins, not only bereft of all things that might obtain favor with God, but laden with many offenses that justly render him terrifying, nevertheless they do not cease to present themselves; and this feeling does not frighten them from betaking themselves to him, since there is no other access to him. For prayer was not ordained that we should be haughtily puffed up before God, or greatly esteem anything of ours, but that, having confessed our guilt, we should deplore our distresses before him, as children unburden their troubles to their parents. Moreover, the boundless mass of our sins should amply furnish us with spurs or goads to arouse us to pray, as the prophet also teaches us by his example: "Heal my soul, for I have sinned against thee" [Ps. 41:4]. I, indeed, confess that in these darts there would be deadly stings if God did not help us. But according to his incomparable compassion, our most gracious Father has added a timely remedy, by which, calming all perturbation, assuaging cares, casting out fears, he may draw us gently to himself—nay, removing all rough spots, not to mention hindrances, he may pave the way.

13. God's command and promise as motive for prayer

First, bidding us pray, by the precept itself he convicts us of impious obstinacy unless we obey. Nothing could be commanded more precisely than what is stated in the psalm: "Call upon me in the day of tribulation" [Ps. 50:15; 49:15, Vg.]. But because among the duties of godliness the Scriptures commend none more frequently, I need not dwell longer on this point. "Seek," says the Master, "and

you will receive; knock, and it will be opened unto you."
[Matt. 7:7.] However, a promise is here also added to the
precept, as is necessary; for even though all admit that the
precept ought to be obeyed, still the majority would flee
from God when he calls if he did not promise to be easily
entreated and readily accessible.

When these two things have been established, it is certain that those who try to wriggle out of coming directly
to God are not only rebellious and stubborn but are also
convicted of unbelief because they distrust the promises.
This is all the more noteworthy, since hypocrites on the
pretense of humility and modesty haughtily despise God's
precept and discredit as well his kindly invitation—even
defraud him of the chief part of his worship. For having
rejected sacrifices in which all holiness then seemed to
rest [Ps. 50:7–13], he declares that to be called upon in the
day of need is highest and precious above all else [Ps.
50:15]. Therefore, when he requires what is his, and spurs
us to eager obedience, there are no colors of doubt, however alluring, that can excuse us. So then, all the passages
that keep occurring in the Scriptures, in which calling
upon God is enjoined upon us, are as so many banners set
up before our eyes to inspire us with confidence. It would
be rashness itself to burst into God's sight if he himself
had not anticipated our coming by calling us. Therefore
he opens a way for us in his own words: "I will say to them,
'You are my people'; they will say to me, 'Thou art our
God'" [Zech. 13:9 p.]. We see how he precedes those who
worship him, and would have them follow him, and thus
not to fear for the sweetness of the melody that he himself dictates.

Especially let that noble title of God come to our minds,
relying upon which we shall without trouble overcome all

obstacles. "O God . . . thou who hearest prayer! To thee shall all flesh come."[Ps. 65:1–2.] For what is more lovely or agreeable than for God to bear this title, which assures us that nothing is more to his nature than to assent to the prayers of suppliants? From this the prophet infers that the door is open not to a few but to all mortals, for he addresses all in these words: "Call upon me in the day of affliction; I will deliver you, and you shall glorify me" [Ps. 50:15]. According to this rule, David claims for himself the promise given him, that he may obtain what he seeks. "Thou, . . . O God, hast revealed to the ear of thy servant . . . ; therefore thy servant has found courage to pray." [2 Sam. 7:27, cf. Vg.] From this we conclude that he was fearful except in so far as the promise had encouraged him. So elsewhere he arms himself with this general doctrine: "He will do the will of those who fear him" [Ps. 145:19; 144:19, Vg.]. Indeed, we may note this in The Psalms: that if the thread of prayer were broken, transition is sometimes made to God's power, sometimes to his goodness, sometimes to the faithfulness of his promises. It might seem that David, by inserting these statements inopportunely, mutilates his prayers, but believers know by use and experience that ardor burns low unless they supply new fuel. Accordingly, among our prayers, meditation both on God's nature and on his Word is by no means superfluous. And so by David's example, let us not disdain to insert something that may refresh our languishing spirits with new vigor.

14. Men should pray confidently, without terror but with reverential fear

It is strange that by promises of such great sweetness we are affected either so coldly or hardly at all, so that many of us prefer to wander through mazes and, forsaking the

fountain of living waters, to dig out for ourselves dry cis-
terns [Jer. 2:13], rather than to embrace God's generosity,
freely given to us. "The name of the Lord is an impreg-
nable citadel," says Solomon; "the righteous man will flee
to it and be saved." [Prov. 18:10 p.] But Joel, after he has
prophesied the frightful ruin that threatens, adds this
memorable sentence: "All that call upon the name of the
Lord shall be delivered" [Joel 2:32; Rom. 10:13]. This we
know actually refers to the course of the gospel [Acts
2:21]. Scarcely one man in a hundred is moved to
approach God. He himself proclaims through Isaiah:
"You will call upon me and I shall hear you. Nay, before
you call, I will answer you" [Isa. 65:24 p.]. Elsewhere he
also vouchsafes this same honor to the whole church in
common, as it applies to all the members of Christ. "He
has called to me and I shall hearken to him; I am with him
in tribulation to rescue him." [Ps. 91:15.] Still, it is not my
purpose, as I have already said, to list every passage but to
choose certain pre-eminent ones, from which we may
taste how gently God attracts us to himself, and with what
tight bonds our ungratefulness is bound when, amidst
such sharp pricks, our sluggishness still delays. Accordingly, let these words ever resound in our ears: "The Lord
is near to all who call upon him, who call upon him in
truth" [Ps. 145:18; cf. 144:18, Vg.]. It is the same with the
words we have quoted from Isaiah and Joel, with which
God assures us that he is attentive to our prayers, and is
even pleased as by a sacrifice of sweet savor when we "cast
our cares upon him" [cf. 1 Peter 5:7; also Ps. 55:22; 54:23,
Vg.]. We receive this singular fruit of God's promises
when we frame our prayers without hesitation or trepida-
tion; but, relying upon the word of him whose majesty
would otherwise terrify us, we dare call upon him as

Father, while he deigns to suggest this sweetest of names to us.

It remains for us, provided with such inducements, to know that we have from this enough evidence that he will hearken to us, inasmuch as our prayers depend upon no merit of ours, but their whole worth and hope of fulfillment are grounded in God's promises, and depend upon them, so that they need no other support, nor do they look about up and down, hither and thither. We must therefore make up our minds that, even though we do not excel in a holiness like that which is praised in the holy patriarchs, prophets, and apostles, yet because we and they have a common command to pray and a common faith, if we rely upon God's Word, in this we are rightly their fellows. For God, as has been seen above, declaring that he will be gentle and kind to all, gives to the utterly miserable, hope that they will get what they have sought. Accordingly, we must note the general forms, by which no one from first to last (as people say) is excluded, provided sincerity of heart, dissatisfaction with ourselves, humility, and faith are present in order that our hypocrisy may not profane God's name by calling upon him deceitfully. Our most gracious Father will not cast out those whom he not only urges, but stirs up with every possible means, to come to him. Hence arises David's way of praying, to which I have recently referred: "Behold, Lord, thou hast promised thy servant, . . . therefore thy servant has today taken heart and found what he might pray before thee. And now, O Lord God, thou art God, and thy words will be true. Thou hast spoken of these benefits to thy servant. Now begin and do it" [2 Sam. 7:27–29, cf. Vg.]. As also elsewhere: "Grant unto thy servant according to thy word." [Ps. 119:76 p.] And all the Israelites together, whenever they arm themselves by remembering the covenant, sufficiently assert that since God so enjoins, one is not to pray fearfully. In this they followed the examples of the patriarchs, especially Jacob, who, after he confessed himself to be less than the many mercies he had received at God's hand [Gen. 32:10], says that he is nevertheless encouraged to ask greater things because God had promised that he would do them [cf. Gen. 32:12–13].

But whatever pretenses unbelievers present, when they do not flee to God whenever necessity presses, do not seek him, and do not implore his help, they defraud him just as much of his due honor as if they made new gods and idols, since in this way they deny God is the author of every good thing. On the other hand, nothing is more effective to free the godly from every misgiving than to be fortified with this thought: there is no reason why any delay should hinder them while they obey the commandment of God, who declares that nothing pleases him more than obedience.

Hence what I have previously said is shown again in clearer light: that a dauntless spirit of praying rightly accords with fear, reverence, and solicitude, and it is not absurd if God raises those who lie prostrate. In this way expressions seemingly discordant beautifully agree. Jeremiah and Daniel say that they lay their prayers before God [Jer. 42:9; Dan. 9:18]. Elsewhere Jeremiah says: "Let our supplication fall before thee that the remnant of thy people may be pitied" [Jer. 42:2 p.]. On the other hand, believers are often said to "lift up prayer." So speaks Hezekiah, when he asks the prophet to intercede on his behalf [2 Kings 19:4]. And David longs to have his prayer rise up "as incense" [Ps. 141:2]. That is, although, persuaded of God's fatherly love, they gladly commit themselves to his safekeeping and do not hesitate to implore the assistance that he freely promises, still they are not elated by heedless confidence, as if they had cast away shame, but they so climb upward by the steps of the promises that they still remain suppliants in their self-abasement.

(God hearkens even to defective prayers, 15–16)
15. Hearkening to perverted prayer

Here more than one question is raised: for Scripture relates that God has granted fulfillment of certain prayers, despite the fact that they have burst forth from a heart not at all peaceful or composed. For due cause, yet aroused by passionate wrath and vengeance, Jotham had vowed the inhabitants of Shechem to the destruction that later overtook them [Judg. 9:20]; God in allowing the curse seems to approve ill-controlled outbreaks. Such passion also seized Samson, when he said: "Strengthen me, O God, that I may take vengeance on the uncircumcised" [Judg. 16:28 p.]. For even though there was some righteous zeal mixed in, still a burning and hence vicious longing for vengeance was in control. God granted the petition. From this, it seems, we may infer that, although prayers are not framed to the rule of the Word, they obtain their effect.

I reply that a universal law is not abrogated by individual examples; further, that special impulses have sometimes been imparted to a few men, by which it came about that a different consideration applied to them than to the common folk. For we must note Christ's answer when his disciples heedlessly desired him to emulate the example of Elijah, that they did not know with what sort of spirit they were endowed [Luke 9:55].

But we must go farther: the prayers that God grants are not always pleasing to him. But in so far as example is concerned, what Scripture teaches is revealed by clear proofs: that he helps the miserable and hearkens to the groans of those who, unjustly afflicted, implore his aid; therefore, that he executes his judgments while complaints of the poor rise up to him, although they are unworthy to receive even a trifle. For how often did he, punishing the cruelty, robberies, violence, lust, and other crimes of the ungodly, silencing their boldness and rage, also overturning their tyrannical power, attest that he helps those wrongly oppressed, who yet beat the air with praying to an unknown god? And one psalm clearly teaches that prayers which do not reach heaven by faith still are not without effect. The psalm lumps together those prayers which, out of natural feeling, necessity wrings from unbelievers just as much as from believers, yet from the outcome it proves that God is gracious toward them [Ps. 107:6, 13, 19]. Is it because he with such gentleness attests the prayers to be acceptable to him? Nay, it is by this circumstance to emphasize or illumine his mercy whenever the prayers of unbelievers are not denied to them; and again to incite his true worshipers to pray the more, when they see that even ungodly wailings sometimes do some good.

Yet there is no reason why believers should turn aside from a law divinely imposed upon them, or should envy unbelievers, as if from having gotten what they wished they had made great gain. We said that in this way God was moved by Ahab's feigned penitence [1 Kings 21:29] in order to prove by this evidence how easily entreated he is toward his elect when they come with true conversion to appease him. Therefore, in Psalm 106, he blames the Jews because, having found him receptive to their pleas [Ps. 106:8–12], they shortly after reverted to the stubbornness of their nature [Ps. 106:43; cf. Ps. 106:13 ff.]. This is also perfectly clear from the history of the Judges: whenever the Israelites wept, even though their tears were false, yet they were rescued from their enemies' hands [cf. Judg. 3:9]. Just as God causes his sun to shine alike upon the good and the evil [Matt. 5:45], so he does not despise the weeping of those whose cause is just and whose distresses deserve to be relieved. Meanwhile, in listening to the prayers of the evil, he no more grants them salvation than he supplies food to those who despise his goodness.

In the cases of Abraham and Samuel, more difficult questions seem to arise—the one, instructed by no word of God, prayed for the people of Sodom [Gen. 18:23]; the other prayed for Saul, even against a downright interdiction [1 Sam. 15:11]. Jeremiah acted similarly when he prayed that the destruction of the city be averted [Jer. 32:16ff.]. For although they suffered a refusal, it seems hard to judge them as not having faith. But this solution, I trust, will satisfy moderate readers: relying upon the general principles by which God bids us bestow mercy even upon the unworthy, they did not utterly lack faith, although in this particular instance their opinion deceived them. Augustine somewhere wisely states: "How do the saints pray in faith when they seek from God what is against his decree? They pray according to his will, not that hidden and unchangeable will but the will that he inspires in them, that he may hearken to them in another way, as he wisely decides." Rightly said. For he so tempers the outcome of events according to his incomprehensible plan that the prayers of the saints, which are a mixture of faith and error, are not nullified. But this ought no more to be held as a valid example for imitation than as excusing the saints themselves; that they exceeded due measure, I do not deny. Therefore, where no certain promise shows

itself, we must ask of God conditionally. Here that statement of David is apposite: "Awake . . . unto the judgment
which thou hast commanded" [Ps. 7:6 p.]. For he shows
that he was instructed by a special oracle to seek a tempo-
ral benefit.

*16. Our prayers can obtain an answer only through God's
forgiveness*

This also is worth noting: what I have set forth on the four
rules of right praying is not so rigorously required that
God will reject those prayers in which he finds neither
perfect faith nor repentance, together with a warmth of
zeal and petitions rightly conceived.

I have said that, although prayer is an intimate conversation of the pious with God, yet reverence and moderation must be kept, lest we give loose rein to miscellaneous
requests, and lest we crave more than God allows; further, that we should lift up our minds to a pure and chaste
veneration of him, lest God's majesty become worthless
for us.

No one has ever carried this out with the uprightness
that was due; for, not to mention the rank and file, how
many complaints of David savor of intemperance! Not
that he would either deliberately expostulate with God or
clamor against his judgments, but that, fainting with
weakness, he finds no other solace better than to cast his
own sorrows into the bosom of God. But God tolerates
even our stammering and pardons our ignorance whenever something inadvertently escapes us; as indeed without this mercy there would be no freedom to pray. But
although David intended to submit completely to God's
will, and prayed with no less patience than zeal to obtain
his request, yet there come forth—sometimes, rather, boil

up—turbulent emotions, quite out of harmony with the first rule that we laid down.

We can especially see from the ending of the Thirty-ninth Psalm with what violent sorrow this holy man is carried away, so that he cannot control himself. "Let me alone," he says, "before I depart, and be no more." [Ps. 39:13, Comm.] One might say that this desperate man seeks nothing except to rot in his evils, with God's hand withdrawn. Not that he deliberately rushes into that intemperance, or, as the wicked are wont, wishes to be far from God, but he only complains that God's wrath is unbearable. In those trials also there are often uttered petitions not sufficiently consonant with the rule of God's Word, and in which the saints do not sufficiently weigh what is lawful and expedient. All prayers marred by these defects deserve to be repudiated; nevertheless, provided the saints bemoan their sins, chastise themselves, and immediately return to themselves, God pardons them.

They likewise sin with regard to the second rule; for they must repeatedly wrestle with their own coldness, and their need and misery do not sharply enough urge them to pray earnestly. Now it often happens that their minds slip away and well-nigh vanish; accordingly, in this respect there is also need for pardon, lest our languid or mutilated, or interrupted and vague, prayers suffer a refusal. God has planted in men's minds by nature the principle that their prayers are lawful only when their minds are uplifted. Hence the rite of lifting up the hands, to which we have previously referred—one common to all ages and peoples, and still in force. But how rarely is there one who, in raising up his hands, is not aware of his own apathy, since his heart stays on the ground?

With regard to seeking forgiveness of sins, although no

believers neglect this topic, yet those truly versed in prayers know that they do not offer the tenth part of that sacrifice of which David speaks: "The sacrifice acceptable to God is a broken spirit; a contrite and humbled heart, O God, thou wilt not despise" [Ps. 51:17, cf. Vg. and Comm.]. Accordingly, men should always seek a twofold pardon because they are aware of many offenses, the feeling of which still does not so touch them that they are as much displeased with themselves as they ought to be, but also because, in so far as it has been granted them to benefit by repentance and fear of God, stricken down with a just sorrow on account of their offenses, they pray that the wrath of the judge be averted.

Most of all it is weakness or imperfection of faith that vitiates believers' prayers, unless God's mercy succor them; but no wonder God pardons this defect, since he often tests his own with sharp trials, as if he deliberately willed to snuff out their faith. Hardest of all is this trial, where believers are compelled to cry out, "How long wilt thou be angry with the prayer of thy servant?" [Ps. 80:4: cf. 79:5, Vg.], as if prayers themselves annoyed God. So when Jeremiah says, "God has shut out my prayer" [Lam. 3:8], there is no doubt that he was stricken with violent perturbation. Innumerable examples of this kind occur in Scripture, from which it is clear the faith of the saints was often so mixed and troubled with doubts that in believing and hoping they yet betrayed some want of faith. But because they do not reach the goal desired, they ought the more to endeavor to correct their faults, and each day come nearer to the perfect rule of prayer. Meanwhile they should feel too the depths of evil in which those have been plunged who bring new diseases upon themselves in their very remedies, seeing that there is no prayer which in justice

God would not loathe if he did not overlook the spots with which all are sprinkled. I do not recount these matters in order that believers may confidently pardon themselves for anything but that by severely chastising themselves they may strive to overcome these obstacles; and although Satan tries to block all paths to prevent them from praying, they should nonetheless break through, surely persuaded that, although not freed of all hindrances, their efforts still please God and their petitions are approved, provided they endeavor and strive toward a goal not immediately attainable.

3.17–20   The Intercession of Christ

When we realize that as sinful persons we are unworthy to present ourselves before God, we can feel shame, fear, and be thrown into despair. But God has given his Son, Jesus Christ, to be our advocate and mediator. This gives us confidence in God's grace! We may approach God in prayer through the name of Jesus Christ, since " 'all God's promises find their yea and amen in him' [2 Cor. 1:20]. That is, they are confirmed and fulfilled" (sec. 17).

In the Old Testament, priests in Israel functioned as mediators between God and the people. The ceremonies where the priests entered the sanctuary and where sacrifices were offered "foreshadow" the work that Jesus Christ performed in the New Testament. We need "a Mediator, who should appear in our name and bear us upon his shoulders and hold us bound upon his breast so that we are heard in his person" (sec. 18). After his ascension to heaven, Christ becomes the church's advocate with God, the "only Mediator, by whose intercession the Father is for us rendered gracious and easily entreated" (secs. 18, 19). Forsaking Christ means we have no access to God.

But Christ is our eternal and abiding mediator. In the church, we pray for one another. As we do, "the mutual prayers for one another of all members yet laboring on earth rise to the Head, who has gone before them into heaven, in whom 'is propitiation for our sins' [1 John 2:2, Vg.]" (sec. 20).

For Reflection and Discussion

1. Why do we need a mediator between us and God?
2. In what ways do Christians benefit from Christ's work of intercession?
3. In what ways are our prayer lives strengthened when we remember that Jesus Christ is our advocate and intercessor?

(The intercession of Christ, 17–20)
17. Prayer in the name of Jesus

Since no man is worthy to present himself to God and come into his sight, the Heavenly Father himself, to free us at once from shame and fear, which might well have thrown our hearts into despair, has given us his Son, Jesus Christ our Lord, to be our advocate [1 John 2:1] and mediator with him [1 Tim. 2:5; cf. Heb. 8:6 and 9:15], by whose guidance we may confidently come to him, and with such an intercessor, trusting nothing we ask in his name will be denied us, as nothing can be denied to him by the Father. And to this must be referred all that we previously taught about faith. For just as the promise commends Christ the Mediator to us, so, unless the hope of obtaining our requests depends upon him, it cuts itself off from the benefit of prayer.

For as soon as God's dread majesty comes to mind, we cannot but tremble and be driven far away by the recognition of our own unworthiness, until Christ comes forward as intermediary, to change the throne of dreadful glory into the throne of grace. As the apostle also teaches how we should dare with all confidence to appear, to receive mercy, and to find grace in timely help [Heb. 4:16]. And as a rule has been established to call upon God, and a promise given that those who call upon him shall be heard, so too we are particularly bidden to call upon him in Christ's name; and we have the promise made that we shall obtain what we have asked in his name. "Hitherto," he says, "you have asked nothing in my name; ask and you will receive." [John 16:24, Comm.] "In that day you will ask in my name" [John 16:26, Vg.], and "whatever you ask . . . I will do it that the Father may be glorified in the Son" [John 14:13, cf. Comm. and Vg.].

Hence it is incontrovertibly clear that those who call

upon God in another name than that of Christ obstinately flout his commands and count his will as nought—indeed, have no promise of obtaining anything. Indeed, as Paul says, "all God's promises find their yea and amen in him" [2 Cor. 1:20]. That is, they are confirmed and fulfilled.

18. The risen Christ as our intercessor

And we ought carefully to note the circumstance of the time when Christ enjoins his disciples to take refuge in his intercession, after he shall have ascended into heaven. "In that hour," he says, "you will ask in my name." [John 16:26.]

It is certain that, from the beginning, those who prayed were not heard save by the Mediator's grace. For this reason, God had taught in the law that the priest alone entering the sanctuary should bear the names of the tribes of Israel upon his shoulders and the same number of precious stones on his breastplate [Ex. 28:9–21], but the people should stand afar off in the court, and there join their petitions with the priest. Nay, the sacrifice even had value in ratifying and strengthening the prayers. Therefore, that foreshadowing ceremony of the law taught us that we are all barred from God's presence, and consequently need a Mediator, who should appear in our name and bear us upon his shoulders and hold us bound upon his breast so that we are heard in his person; further, that our prayers are cleansed by sprinkled blood—prayers that, as has been stated, are otherwise never free of uncleanness. And we see that the saints, when they desired to obtain something, based their hope on sacrifices, for they knew them to be the sanctions of all petitions. "May he remember your offering," says David, "and make your burnt sacrifice fat!" [Ps. 20:3 p., cf. Comm.] Hence we infer that God was from the beginning appeased by Christ's intercession, so that he received the petitions of the godly.

Why, then, does Christ assign a new hour wherein his disciples shall begin to pray in his name unless it is that this grace, as it is more resplendent today, so deserves more approval among us? And he had said a little before in the same sense: "Hitherto you have asked nothing in my name; ask" [John 16:24]. Not that they understand absolutely nothing about the office of Mediator, since all the Jews were steeped in these rudiments, but because they did not yet clearly understand that Christ by his very ascension into heaven would be a surer advocate of the church than he had been before. Therefore, to console their grief at his absence with some uncommon benefit, he takes upon himself the office of advocate, and teaches that they had hitherto lacked the peculiar blessing that will be given them to enjoy when, relying upon his protection, they more freely call upon God. Thus the apostle says that the new way is consecrated by his blood [Heb. 10:20]. The less excusable is our frowardness unless we embrace with both arms, as the saying is, this truly inestimable benefit, which is destined for us alone.

19. Christ is the only Mediator, even for the mutual intercession of believers
Now, since he is the only way, and the one access, by which it is granted us to come to God [cf. John 14:6], to those who turn aside from this way and forsake this access, no way and no access to God remain; nothing is left in his throne but wrath, judgment, and terror. Moreover, since the Father has sealed him [cf. John 6:27] as our Head [Matt. 2:6] and Leader [1 Cor. 11:3; Eph. 1:22; 4:15; 5:23; Col. 1:18], those who in any way turn aside or incline away

from him are trying their level best to destroy and disfigure the mark imprinted by God. Thus Christ is constituted the only Mediator, by whose intercession the Father is for us rendered gracious and easily entreated.

Meanwhile, notwithstanding, the saints still retain their intercessions, whereby they commend one another's salvation to God. The apostle mentions these [1 Tim. 2:1], but all depend solely upon Christ's intercession, so far are they from detracting from his in any way. For as they gush forth from the emotion of love, in which we willingly and freely embrace one another as members of one body, so also are they related to the unity of the Head. When, therefore, those intercessions are also made in Christ's name, what else do they attest but that no one can be helped by any prayers at all save when Christ intercedes? Christ does not by his intercession hinder us from pleading for one another by prayers in the church. So, then, let it remain an established principle that we should direct all intercessions of the whole church to that sole intercession. Indeed, especially for this reason should we beware of ungratefulness, because God, pardoning our unworthiness, not only allows individuals to pray for themselves but also permits men to plead for one another. For when God has appointed advocates of his church who deserve to be duly rejected if each one prays exclusively for himself, what sheer presumption is it to abuse this generosity so as to dim Christ's honor?

20. Christ is the eternal and abiding Mediator

This babbling of the Sophists is mere nonsense: that Christ is the Mediator of redemption, but believers are mediators of intercession. As if Christ had performed a mediation in time only to lay upon his servants the eternal and undying mediation! They who cut off so slight a portion of honor from him are, of course, treating him gently! Yet Scripture speaks far differently, disregarding these deceivers, and with a simplicity that ought to satisfy a godly man. For when John says, "If anyone sins, we have an advocate with the Father, Christ Jesus" [1 John 2:1], does he mean that Christ was an advocate for us once for all, or does he not rather ascribe to him a constant intercession? Why does Paul affirm that he "sits at the right hand of the Father and also intercedes for us" [Rom. 8:34 p.]? But when, in another passage, Paul calls him "the sole mediator between God and man" [1 Tim. 2:5], is he not referring to prayers, which were mentioned shortly before [1 Tim. 2:1–2]? For, after previously saying that intercession is to be made for all men, Paul, to prove this statement, soon adds that "there is one God, and . . . one mediator" [1 Tim. 2:5].

Augustine similarly explains it when he says: "Christian men mutually commend one another by their prayers. However, it is he for whom no one intercedes, while he intercedes for all, who is the one true Mediator." The apostle Paul, although an eminent member under the Head, yet because he was a member of Christ's body, and knew that the greatest and truest priest of the church had not figuratively entered the inner precincts of the veil to the Holy of Holies but through express and steadfast truth had entered the inner precincts of heaven to a holiness real and eternal, also commends himself to the prayers of believers [Rom. 15:30; Eph. 6:19; Col. 4:3]. And he does not make himself mediator between the people and God, but he asks that all members of Christ's body mutually pray for one another, "since the members are concerned for one another, and if one member suffers, the rest suffer with it" [1 Cor. 12:25–26, cf. Vg.]. And thus the mutual prayers for one another of all members yet laboring on earth rise to the Head, who has gone before them into heaven, in whom "is propitiation for our sins" [1 John 2:2, Vg.]. For if Paul were mediator, so also would the rest of the apostles be; and if there were many mediators, Paul's own statement would not stand, in which he had said: "One God, one mediator between God and men, the man Christ" [1 Tim. 2:5], "in whom we also are one" [Rom. 12:5], "if we maintain unity of faith in the bond of peace" [Eph. 4:3]. Likewise, in another passage Augustine says: "But if you seek a priest, he is above the heavens, where he is making intercession for you, who died for you on earth." [Cf. Heb. 7:26ff.]

But we do not imagine that he, kneeling before God, pleads as a suppliant for us; rather, with the apostle we understand he so appears before God's presence that the power of his death avails as an everlasting intercession in our behalf [cf. Rom. 8:34], yet in such a way that, having entered the heavenly sanctuary, even to the consummation of the ages [cf. Heb. 9:24ff.], he alone bears to God the petitions of the people, who stay far off in the outer court.

(*Rejection of erroneous doctrines of the intercession of saints, 21–27*)

3.20.28–30   Kinds of Prayer: Private and Public

Our prayers are composed of petition and thanksgiving. In petition, we pour out our desires to God, seeking "both those things which make for the extension of his glory and the setting forth of his name, and those benefits which conduce to our own advantage." When we give thanks, we "celebrate with due praise his benefits toward us, and credit to his generosity every good that comes to us" (sec. 28). Both these types of prayers are important.

Since God is the author of all blessings, praise and thanksgiving should be constants in the Christian life. If we fail to offer praise to God, says Calvin, "our silence is spiteful." As often as God blesses us, we have the opportunities to offer praise. Paul says we are to pray and give thanks to God "without ceasing" (1 Thess. 5:17; sec. 28).

We pray in private and in public. We must always guard against "vain repetitions" in prayer—thinking that we can gain something from God by "beating upon his ears with a garrulous flow of talk" (sec. 29). We must never offer prayers to draw attention to ourselves. Instead, true prayer proceeds from the heart since "prayer itself is properly an emotion of the heart within, which is poured out and laid open before God, the searcher of hearts ([cf. Rom. 8:27]" (sec. 29).

For Reflection and Discussion

1. Do you find it easier to offer prayers of petition or thanksgiving? Are both types part of your life of prayer?

2. Calvin says we are overwhelmed by so many benefits from God and "by so many and mighty miracles discerned wherever one looks" that we "never lack reason and occasion for praise and thanksgiving." What benefits and "miracles" have you received?

3. Calvin says that we ourselves are "God's true temples," rather than church buildings. In what ways do you see yourself and others in the church as "God's true temples"?

(Kinds of prayer: private and public, 28–30)
28. Private prayer

But even though prayer is properly confined to entreaties and supplications, there is such a close connection between petition and thanksgiving that they may conveniently be included under one name. For those kinds which Paul lists fall under the first part of this division [cf.1 Tim. 2:1]. In asking and beseeching, we pour out our desires before God, seeking both those things which make for the extension of his glory and the setting forth of his name, and those benefits which conduce to our own advantage. In giving thanks, we celebrate with due praise his benefits toward us, and credit to his generosity every good that comes to us. David, therefore, has combined these two functions: "Call upon me in the day of need; I will deliver you, and you shall glorify me" [Ps. 50:15]. Scripture with good reason enjoins us to use both constantly. For as we have stated elsewhere, the weight of our poverty and the facts of experience proclaim that the tribulations which drive and press us from all sides are so many and so great that there is reason enough for us all continually to groan and sigh to God, and to beseech him as suppliants, For even if they be free of adversities, the guilt of their transgressions and the innumerable assaults of temptations ought still to goad even the holiest to seek a remedy. But in the sacrifice of praise and thanksgiving there can be no interruption without sin, since God does not cease to heap benefits upon benefits in order to impel us, though slow and lazy, to gratefulness. In short, we are well-nigh overwhelmed by so great and so plenteous an outpouring of benefactions, by so many and mighty miracles discerned wherever one looks, that we never lack reason and occasion for praise and thanksgiving.

And to explain these things somewhat more clearly, since, as has already been sufficiently proved, all our hope and wealth so reside in God that neither we nor our possessions prosper unless we can have his blessing, we ought constantly to commit ourselves and all that we have to him [cf. James 4:14–15]. Then whatever we determine, speak, do, let us determine, speak, and do under his hand and will—in a word, under the hope of his help. For all are declared accursed by God who, placing confidence in themselves or someone else, conceive and carry out their plans; who undertake or try to begin anything apart from his will, and without calling upon him [cf. Isa. 30:1; 31:1]. And since, as we have said several times, he is honored in the manner due him when he is acknowledged the author of all blessings, it follows that we ought so to receive all those things from his hand as to accompany them with continual thanksgiving; and that there is no just reason for us to make use of his benefits, which flow and come to us from his generosity, with no other end, if we do not continually utter his praise and render him thanks. For Paul, when he testifies that they "are sanctified by the word . . . and prayer" [1 Tim. 4:5], at the same time hints that without the word and prayer they are not at all holy and pure for us. ("Word" he evidently understands, by metonymy, as "faith.") Accordingly, David, when he has perceived the Lord's generosity, beautifully declares a "new song" has been put into his mouth [Ps. 40:3]. By this he naturally hints that if we fail to offer him praise for his blessing, our silence is spiteful, since as often as he blesses us he provides us with occasion to bless him. So Isaiah also, proclaiming God's singular grace, urges believers to a new and uncommon song [Isa. 42:10]. In this sense, David elsewhere speaks: "O Lord, open thou my lips, and my mouth shall show forth thy praise" [Ps. 51:15; 50:17, Vg.]. In like manner, Hezekiah and Jonah testify that this will be the outcome of their deliverance: that they may sing the praises of God's goodness in the Temple [Isa. 38:20; Jonah 2:9]. David prescribes the same rule to all the godly in common. "What shall I render to the Lord," he says, "for all his bounty to me? I will lift up the cup of salvation and call on the name of the Lord." [Ps. 116:12–13; cf. Comm. and 115:l2–13, Vg.] And the church follows this rule in another psalm: "Make us safe, O our God, . . . that we may confess thy . . . name, and glory in thy praise" [Ps. 106:47; 105:47, Vg.]. Again: "He has had regard for the prayer of the solitary, and has not despised their prayers. This will be written for a later generation, and the people created shall praise the Lord . . . to proclaim his name in Zion, and his praise in Jerusalem" [Ps. 102:17, 18 (Comm.), 21; cf. Ps. 101:21, Vg. and LXX]. Indeed, whenever believers entreat God to do something for his name's sake, as they profess themselves unworthy to obtain anything in their own name, so they obligate themselves to give thanks; and they promise that they will rightly use God's benefit, to be the heralds of it. So Hosea, speaking of the coming redemption of the church: "Take away," he says, "iniquity, O God, and accept that which is good, and we will render the bullocks of our lips" [Hos. 14:3, Vg., see Comm.].

Not only do God's benefits claim for themselves the extolling by the tongue, but also they naturally win love for themselves. "I loved the Lord," says David, "because he heard the voice of my supplication." [Ps. 116:1; cf. Comm. and Ps. 115:15, Vg.] Also, elsewhere recounting what help he had experienced: "I shall love thee, O God, my strength" [Ps. 18:1 p.]. But praises that do not flow from this sweetness of love will never please God. Even more, we must understand Paul's statement that all entreaties not joined with thanksgiving are wicked and vicious. For he speaks thus: "In all prayer," he says, "and supplication with thanksgiving let your petitions be made known to God" [Phil. 4:6 p.]. For since many by peevishness, boredom, impatience, bitter grief, and fear are impelled to mumble when praying, he bids believers so to temper their emotions that while still waiting to obtain what they desire, they nonetheless cheerfully bless God. But if this connection ought to be in full force in things almost contrary, by a still holier bond God obligates us to sing his praises whenever he causes us to obtain our wishes.

Now even as we have taught that by Christ's intercession are consecrated our prayers, which would otherwise have been unclean, so the apostle, enjoining us to offer a sacrifice of praise through Christ [Heb. 13:15], warns us that our mouths are not clean enough to sing the praises of God's name until Christ's priesthood intercedes for us. We infer from this that in the papacy men have been strangely bewitched, since the majority of them wonder why Christ is called "the Advocate."

The reason why Paul enjoins us both to pray and to give thanks without ceasing [1 Thess. 5:17–18; cf. 1 Tim. 2:1, 8] is, of course, that he wishes all men to lift up their desires to God, with all possible constancy, at all times, in all places, and in all affairs and transactions, to expect all things from him, and give him praise for all things, since he offers us unfailing reasons to praise and pray.

29. Necessity and danger of public prayer

This constancy in prayer, even though it has especially to do with one's own private prayers, still is also concerned somewhat with the public prayers of the church. Yet these can neither be constant nor ought they even to take place otherwise than according to the polity agreed upon by common consent among all. This I grant you. For this reason, certain hours, indifferent to God but necessary for men's convenience, are agreed upon and appointed to provide for the accommodation of all, and for everything to be done "decently and in order" in the church, according to Paul's statement [1 Cor. 14:40]. But this does not preclude each church from being both repeatedly stirred up to more frequent use of prayer and fired by a sharper zeal if it is alerted by some major need. There will be, moreover, toward the end, a place to speak of perseverance, which has close affinity with constancy.

Now these matters have nothing to do with the vain repetition that Christ willed to be forbidden to us [Matt. 6:7]. For Christ does not forbid us to persist in prayers, long, often, or with much feeling, but requires that we should not be confident in our ability to wrest something from God by beating upon his ears with a garrulous flow of talk, as if he could be persuaded as men are. For we know that hypocrites, because they do not reflect that they have to do with God, make the same pompous show in prayers as they would in a triumph. For that Pharisee who thanked God that he was not like other men [Luke 18:11] doubtless praised himself in men's eyes, as if he would from praying latch on to renown for holiness. Hence that vain repetition which for a similar reason is in vogue today in the papacy. While some pass the time in saying over and over the same little prayers, others vaunt themselves before the crowd with a great mass of words. Since this talkativeness childishly mocks God, it is no wonder that it is forbidden by the church in order that nothing shall resound there except what is earnest and comes forth from the depths of the heart.

Near and similar to this corrupt element is another, which Christ condemns at the same time: hypocrites, for the sake of show, pant after many witnesses, and would rather frequent the market place to pray than have their prayers miss the world's applause [Matt. 6:5]. But inasmuch as this goal of prayer has already been stated—namely, that hearts may be aroused and borne to God, whether to praise him or to beseech his help—from this we may understand that the essentials of prayer are set in the mind and heart, or rather that prayer itself is properly an emotion of the heart within, which is poured out and laid open before God, the searcher of hearts [cf. Rom. 8:27]. Accordingly, as has already been said, the Heavenly Teacher, when he willed to lay down the best rule for prayer, bade us enter into our bedroom and there, with door closed, pray to our Father in secret, that our Father, who is in secret, may hear us [Matt. 6:6]. For, when he has drawn us away from the example of hypocrites, who grasped after the favor of men by vain and ostentatious prayers, he at the same time adds something better: that is, to enter into our bedroom and there, with door closed, pray. By these words, as I understand them, he taught us to seek a retreat that would help us to descend into our heart with our whole thought and enter deeply within. He promises that God, whose temples our bodies ought to be, will be near to us in the affections of our hearts [cf. 2 Cor. 6:16].

For he did not mean to deny that it is fitting to pray in other places, but he shows that prayer is something secret, which is both principally lodged in the heart and requires a tranquillity far from all our teeming cares. The Lord himself also, therefore, with good reason, when he determined to devote himself more intensely to prayers, habitually withdrew to a quiet spot far away from the tumult of men; but he did so to impress us with his example that we must not neglect these helps, whereby our mind, too unsteady by itself, more inclines to earnest application to prayer. In the meantime, as he did not abstain from praying even in the midst of a crowd if the occasion so presented itself, so we should lift up clean hands in all places, where there is need [1 Tim. 2:8]. Finally, we must consider that whoever refused to pray in the holy assembly of the godly knows not what it is to pray individually, or in a secret spot, or at home. Again, he who neglects to pray alone and in private, however unremittingly he may frequent public assemblies, there contrives only windy prayers, for he defers more to the opinion of men than to the secret judgment of God.

Moreover, that the common prayers of the church may not be held in contempt, God of old adorned them with shining titles, especially when he called the temple the "house of prayer" [Isa. 56:7; Matt. 21:13]. For he taught by this term that the chief part of his worship lies in the office of prayer, and that the temple was set up like a banner for believers so that they might, with one consent, participate in it. A distinctive promise was also added: "Praise waits for thee, O God, in Zion, and to thee shall the vow be performed" [Ps. 65:1, Comm.]. By these words the prophet intimates that the prayers of the church are never ineffectual, for God always furnishes his people occasion for singing with joy. But even though the shadows of the law have ceased, still there is no doubt that the same promise pertains to us, since God was pleased by this ceremony to foster the unity of the faith among us. For not only has Christ sanctioned this promise by his own mouth, but Paul holds it to be universally in force.

30. Not church buildings but we ourselves are temples of God

Now as God by his word ordains common prayers for believers, so also ought there to be public temples wherein these may be performed, in which those who spurn fellowship with God's people in prayer have no occasion to give the false excuse that they enter their bedroom to obey the Lord's command. For he, who promises that he will do whatever two or three gathered together in his name may ask [Matt. 18:19–20], testifies that he does not despise prayers publicly made, provided ostentation and chasing after paltry human glory are banished, and there is present a sincere and true affection that dwells in the secret place of the heart.

If this is the lawful use of church buildings, as it certainly is, we in turn must guard against either taking them to be God's proper dwelling places, whence he may more nearly incline his ear to us—as they began to be regarded some centuries ago—or feigning for them some secret holiness or other, which would render prayer more sacred before God. For since we ourselves are God's true temples, if we would call upon God in his holy temple, we must pray within ourselves. Now let us leave this stupidity to Jews or pagans, for we have the commandment to call upon the Lord, without distinction of place, "in spirit and in truth" [John 4:23]. At God's command the Temple had indeed been dedicated of old for offering prayers and sacrificial victims, but at that time the truth lay hidden, figuratively represented under such shadows; now, having been expressed to us in living reality, it does not allow us to cleave to any material temple. And not even to the Jews was the Temple committed on the condition that they might shut up God's presence within its walls but in order that they might be trained to contemplate the likeness of the true temple. Therefore Isaiah and Stephen gravely rebuked those who thought God in any way dwells in temples made with hands [Isa. 66:1; Acts 7:48–49].

3.20.31–33   The Use of Singing, and of the Spoken Language

Calvin strongly commends speaking and singing in prayer, saying that the tongue has been assigned the task of proclaiming the glory of God, for "it was peculiarly created to tell and proclaim the praise of God." All prayer and all singing, however, must "spring from deep feeling of heart." Voice and song must be united as expressions of the "heart's affection" (sec. 31).

Church singing, which has been part of Christian worship since the early church, should be encouraged. It "both lends dignity and grace to sacred actions and has the greatest value in kindling our hearts to a true zeal and eagerness to pray." Yet Calvin cites a danger and issues a warning that "we should be very careful that our ears be not more attentive to the melody than our minds to the spiritual meaning of the words." Singing can be "a most holy and salutary practice." Yet, "such songs as have been composed only for sweetness and delight of the ear are unbecoming to the majesty of the church and cannot but displease God in the highest degree" (sec. 32).

Public prayers, says Calvin, should be in the language of the people and offered for "the edification of the whole church." Tongue and mind should join in prayer. When feelings of mind are aroused, "the tongue breaks forth into speech, and the other members into gesture." Kneeling and other bodily gestures attempt to show greater reverence for God (sec. 33).

For Reflection and Discussion

1. In what ways do you use your tongue to "tell and proclaim the praise of God"?
2. What benefits do you believe singing in church provides?
3. Are there bodily gestures or practices you use to enhance your expression of reverence for God?

(The use of singing, and of the spoken language, 31–33)
31. On speaking and singing in prayer

From this, moreover, it is fully evident that unless voice and song, if interposed in prayer, spring from deep feeling of heart, neither has any value or profit in the least with God. But they arouse his wrath against us if they come only from the tip of the lips and from the throat, seeing that this is to abuse his most holy name and to hold his majesty in derision. This is what we gather from Isaiah's words, which, although they extend farther, also are concerned with reproving this fault. "The people," he says, "draw near to me with their mouth, and honor me with their lips, but their hearts are far from me, and they have feared me by the command and teaching of men." [Isa. 29:13; cf. Matt. 15:8–9.] "Therefore, behold, I will . . . do a great and marvelous miracle among this people; for the wisdom of their wise men shall perish, and the prudence of their elders shall vanish." [Isa. 29:14 p., cf. Vg.]

Yet we do not here condemn speaking and singing but rather strongly commend them, provided they are associated with the heart's affection. For thus do they exercise the mind in thinking of God and keep it attentive—unstable and variable as it is, and readily relaxed and diverted in different directions, unless it be supported by various helps. Moreover, since the glory of God ought, in a measure, to shine in the several parts of our bodies, it is especially fitting that the tongue has been assigned and destined for this task, both through singing and through speaking. For it was peculiarly created to tell and proclaim the praise of God. But the chief use of the tongue is in public prayers, which are offered in the assembly of believers, by which it comes about that with one common voice, and as it were, with the same mouth, we all glorify God together, worshiping him with one spirit and the same faith. And we do this openly, that all men mutually, each one from his brother, may receive the confession of faith and be invited and prompted by his example.

32. Church singing

It is evident that the practice of singing in church, to speak also of this in passing, is not only a very ancient one but also was in use among the apostles. This we may infer from Paul's words: "I will sing with the spirit and I will sing with the mind" [1 Cor. 14:15]. Likewise, Paul speaks to the Colossians: "Teaching and admonishing one another . . . in hymns, psalms, and spiritual songs, singing with thankfulness in your hearts to the Lord." [Col. 3:16 p.] For in the first passage he teaches that we should sing with voice and heart; in the second he commends spiritual songs, by which the godly may mutually edify one another.

Yet Augustine testifies that this practice was not universal when he states that the church of Milan first began to sing only under Ambrose; the occasion being that when Justina, the mother of Valentinian, was raging against the orthodox faith, the people were more constant in vigils than usual. Then the remaining Western churches followed Milan. For a little before he had said that this custom had come from the Eastern churches. He also indicates in the second book of his *Retractations* that the practice was taken up in Africa in his day. "A certain Hilary," he says, "an ex-tribune, attacked with malicious reproof, wherever he could, the custom, then just begun at Carthage, of singing hymns from the book of Psalms at the altar, either before the offering or when what had been offered was being distributed to the people. At the bidding of my brethren, I answered him."

And surely, if the singing be tempered to that gravity which is fitting in the sight of God and the angels, it both lends dignity and grace to sacred actions and has the greatest value in kindling our hearts to a true zeal and eagerness to pray. Yet we should be very careful that our ears be not more attentive to the melody than our minds to the spiritual meaning of the words. Augustine also admits in another place that he was so disturbed by this danger that he sometimes wished to see established the custom observed by Athanasius, who ordered the reader to use so little inflection of the voice that he would sound more like a speaker than a singer. But when he recalled how much benefit singing had brought him, he inclined to the other side. Therefore, when this moderation is maintained, it is without any doubt a most holy and salutary practice. On the other hand, such songs as have been composed only for sweetness and delight of the ear are unbecoming to the majesty of the church and cannot but displease God in the highest degree.

33. *Prayer should be in the language of the people*

From this also it plainly appears that public prayers must be couched not in Greek among the Latins, nor in Latin among the French or English, as has heretofore been the custom, but in the language of the people, which can be generally understood by the whole assembly. For this ought to be done for the edification of the whole church, which receives no benefit whatever from a sound not understood. Those who have no regard for either love or kindliness ought at least to have been moved a little by the authority of Paul, whose words are perfectly clear. "If you bless with the spirit," he says, "how can he who occupies the place of the unlearned respond to your blessing with 'Amen,' since he is ignorant of what you are saying? For you indeed give thanks, but the other is not edified."

[1 Cor. 14:16–17 p.] Who can marvel enough, then, at the unbridled license of the papists, who, after the apostle thus openly decries it, are not afraid to make their wordy prayers resound in a foreign language, of which they themselves often understand not one syllable, and do not wish others to understand either?

But for us Paul prescribes otherwise what is to be done. "What am I to do?" he says. "I will pray with the spirit, I will pray with the mind also; I will sing with the spirit and I will sing with the mind also." [1 Cor. 4:15.] By the word "spirit" he means the singular gift of tongues, which some, though endowed therewith, abused, since they cut it off from the mind, that is, the understanding. However, we must unquestionably feel that, either in public prayer or in private, the tongue without the mind must be highly displeasing to God. Besides, the mind ought to be kindled with an ardor of thought so as far to surpass all that the tongue can express by speaking.

Lastly, we should hold that the tongue is not even necessary for private prayer, except in so far as either the inner feeling has insufficient power to arouse itself or as it is so vehemently aroused that it carries with it the action of the tongue. For even though the best prayers are sometimes unspoken, it often happens in practice that, when feelings of mind are aroused, unostentatiously the tongue breaks forth into speech, and the other members into gesture. From this obviously arose that uncertain murmur of Hannah's [1 Sam. 1:13], something similar to which all the saints continually experience when they burst forth into broken and fragmentary speech.

As for the bodily gestures customarily observed in praying, such as kneeling and uncovering the head, they are exercises whereby we try to rise to a greater reverence for God.

3.20.34–43   The Lord's Prayer: Exposition of the First Three Petitions

Jesus Christ has provided us with a "right pattern for prayer" through which we can acknowledge God's "goodness and clemency" and which enables us to seek God in our "every need, as children are wont to take refuge in the protection of the parents whenever they are troubled with any anxiety" (sec. 34). The first three petitions of the Lord's Prayer are concerned with God's glory; the last three, with "the care of ourselves" (sec. 35).

We can address God as "Our Father" because we have been "adopted as children of grace in Christ" (sec. 36). We approach God as children to their parent, assured that God who is the loving parent (Luke 15:11–32) is "*our*" Father" (sec. 37). Love for others should be stirred by addressing God this way since "we are equally children" of this loving God. Christians should embrace all persons as children of God since what God does in their lives is "beyond our knowing except that it is no less godly than humane to wish and hope the best for them" (sec. 38).

We pray that God's name be hallowed—to give honor to God and think of God with the highest reverence (sec. 41). We pray for God's kingdom to come—God's reign to be established (sec. 42). We pray for God's will to be done on earth as in heaven—an end to "all arrogance and wickedness" and the earth subject to God's rule and "all peace and uprightness" to prevail (see 43).

For Reflection and Discussion

1 What are implications of Jesus' using "our" instead of "my" to address God?
2. In what ways can we "hallow" or show reverence for God's name?
3. Do you believe it is possible for humans to establish God's reign by our own obedience? Why or why not?

*(The Lord's Prayer: exposition of the first three petitions,
34–43)*

34. The Lord's Prayer as necessary help for us

Now we must learn not only a more certain way of praying but also the form itself: namely, that which the Heavenly Father has taught us through his beloved Son [Matt.
6:9ff.; Luke 11:2ff.], in which we may acknowledge his
boundless goodness and clemency. For he warns us and
urges us to seek him in our every need, as children are
wont to take refuge in the protection of the parents whenever they are troubled with any anxiety. Besides this, since
he saw that we did not even sufficiently perceive how
straitened our poverty was, what it was fair to request, and
what was profitable for us, he also provided for this ignorance of ours; and what had been lacking to our capacity
he himself supplied and made sufficient from his own. For
he prescribed a form for us in which he set forth as in a
table all that he allows us to seek of him, all that is of benefit to us, all that we need ask. From this kindness of his
we receive great fruit of consolation: that we know we are
requesting nothing absurd, nothing strange or unseemly—
in short, nothing unacceptable to him—since we are asking almost in his own words. Plato, on seeing men's want
of skill in making requests to God, which, if granted,
would often have been disadvantageous to them, declares
this, taken from an ancient poet, to be the best prayer:
"King Jupiter, bestow the best things upon us whether we
wish for them or not, but command that evil things be far
from us even when we request them." And, indeed, the
heathen man is wise in that he judges how dangerous it is
to seek from the Lord what our greed dictates; at the same
time he discloses our unhappiness, in that we cannot even
open our mouths before God without danger unless the
Spirit instructs us in the right pattern for prayer [Rom.
8:26]. This privilege deserves to be more highly esteemed

among us, since the only-begotten Son of God supplies words to our lips that free our minds from all wavering.

35. Division and main content

This form or rule of prayer consists of six petitions. The reason why I do not agree with those who distinguish seven headings is that by inserting the adversative "but" the Evangelist seems to have meant to join those two members together. It is as if he had said: "Do not allow us to be oppressed by temptation but rather bring help for our weakness, and deliver us from falling." Ancient writers of the church also agree with us, so that what has been added in seventh place in Matthew exegetically ought to be referred to the sixth petition.

But even though the whole prayer is such that throughout it God's glory is to be given chief place, still the first three petitions have been particularly assigned to God's glory, and this alone we ought to look to in them, without consideration of what is called our own advantage. The three others are concerned with the care of ourselves, and are especially assigned to those things which we should ask for our own benefit. So, when we ask that God's name be hallowed, because God wills to test us whether we love and worship him freely or for hope of reward, we must then have no consideration for our own benefit but must set before ourselves his glory, to gaze with eyes intent upon this one thing. And in the remaining petitions of this sort, it is meet to be affected in precisely the same way.

And, indeed, this yields a great benefit to us, because when his name is hallowed as we ask, our own hallowing in turn also comes about. But our eyes ought, as it were, to be closed and in a sense blinded to this sort of advantage, so that they have no regard for it at all, and so that, if all hope of our own private good were cut off, still we should not cease to desire and entreat this hallowing and the other things that pertain to God's glory. In the examples of Moses and Paul, we see that it was not grievous for them to turn their minds and eyes away from themselves and to long for their own destruction with fierce and burning zeal in order that, despite their own loss, they might advance God's glory and Kingdom [Ex. 32:32; Rom. 9:3]. On the other hand, when we ask to be given our daily bread, even though we desire what is to our benefit, here also we ought especially to seek God's glory so as not to ask it unless it redound to his glory. Now let us turn to the interpretation of the prayer.

(*"Our Father, who art in heaven"*)
36. *"Our Father"*
First, at the very threshold we meet what I previously mentioned: we ought to offer all prayer to God only in Christ's name, as it cannot be agreeable to him in any other name. For in calling God "Father," we put forward the name "Christ." With what confidence would anyone address God as "Father"? Who would break forth into such rashness as to claim for himself the honor of a son of God unless we had been adopted as children of grace in Christ? He, while he is the true Son, has of himself been given us as a brother that what he has of his own by nature may become ours by benefit of adoption if we embrace this great blessing with sure faith. Accordingly, John says that power has been given to those who believe in the name of the only-begotten Son of God, that they too may become children of God [John 1:12].

Therefore God both calls himself our Father and would have us so address him. By the great sweetness of this name he frees us from all distrust, since no greater feeling of love can be found elsewhere than in the Father. Therefore he could not attest his own boundless love toward us with any surer proof than the fact that we are called "children of God" [1 John 3:1]. But just as he surpasses all men in goodness and mercy, so is his love greater and more excellent than all our parents' love. Hence, though all earthly fathers should divest themselves of all feeling of fatherhood and forsake their children, he will never fail us [cf. Ps. 27:10; Isa. 63:16], since he cannot deny himself [2 Tim. 2:13]. For we have his promise: "If you, although you are evil, know how to give good gifts to your children, how much more will your Father, who is in heaven" [Matt. 7:11 p.]? Similarly, in the prophet: "Can a woman forget her . . . children? . . . Even if she forgets, yet I shall not forget you." [Isa. 49:15 p.] But a son cannot give himself over to the safekeeping of a stranger and an alien without at the same time complaining either of his father's cruelty or want. Thus, if we are his sons, we cannot seek help anywhere else than from him without reproaching him for poverty, or want of means, or cruelty and excessive rigor.

37. *"Our Father": a form of address that should encourage us*

And let us not pretend that we are justly rendered timid by the consciousness of sins, since sins daily make our Father, although kind and gentle, displeased with us. For if among men, a son can have no better advocate to plead his cause before his father, can have no better intermediary to conciliate and recover his lost favor, than if he himself, suppliant and humble, acknowledging his guilt, implores his father's mercy—for then his father's heart cannot pretend to be moved by such entreaties—what will he do who is the Father of mercies and God of all comfort [cf. 2 Cor. 1:3]? Will he not rather heed the tears and groans of his children entreating for themselves, since he particularly invites and exhorts us to this, than any pleas of others, to whose help they in terror have recourse, not without some signs of despair, since they are distrustful of their Father's compassion and kindness? He depicts and represents for us in a parable [Luke 15:11–32] this abundance of fatherly compassion: a son had estranged himself from his father, had dissolutely wasted his substance [v. 13], had grievously offended against him in every way [v. 18]; but the father embraces him with open arms, and does not wait for him to ask for pardon but anticipates him, recognizes him returning afar off, willingly runs to meet him [v. 20], comforts him, receives him into favor [vv. 22–24]. For in setting forth this example of great compassion to be seen in man, he willed to teach us how much more abundantly we ought to expect it of him. For he is not only a father but by far the best and kindest of all fathers, provided we still cast ourselves upon his mercy, although we are ungrateful, rebellious, and froward children. And to strengthen our assurance that he is this sort of father to us if we are Christians, he willed that we call him not only "Father" but explicitly "our Father." It is as if we addressed him: "O Father, who dost abound with great devotion toward thy children, and with great readiness to forgive, we thy children call upon thee and make our prayer, assured and clearly persuaded that thou bearest toward us only the affection of a father, although we are unworthy of such a father."

But because the narrowness of our hearts cannot comprehend God's boundless favor, not only is Christ the pledge and guarantee of our adoption, but he gives the

Spirit as witness to us of the same adoption, through whom with free and full voice we may cry, "Abba, Father" [Gal. 4:6; Rom. 8:15]. Therefore, whenever any hesitation shall hinder us, let us remember to ask him to correct our fearfulness, and to set before us that Spirit that he may guide us to pray boldly.

38. "Our Father": A form of address that sets us in the fellowship with the brethren

However, we are not so instructed that each one of us should individually call him *his Father*, but rather that all of us in common should call him *our Father*. From this fact we are warned how great a feeling of brotherly love ought to be among us, since by the same right of mercy and free liberality we are equally children of such a father. For if one father is common to us all [Matt. 23:9], and every good thing that can fall to our lot comes from him, there ought not to be anything separate among us that we are not prepared gladly and wholeheartedly to share with one another, as far as occasion requires.

Now if we so desire, as is fitting, to extend our hand to one another and to help one another, there is nothing in which we can benefit our brethren more than in commending them to the providential care of the best of fathers; for if he is kind and favorable, nothing at all else can be desired. Indeed, we owe even this very thing to our Father. Just as one who truly and deeply loves any father of a family at the same time embraces his whole household with love and good will, so it becomes us in like measure to show to his people, to his family, and lastly, to his inheritance, the same zeal and affection that we have toward this Heavenly Father. For he so honored these as to call them the fullness of his only-begotten Son [Eph. 1:23].

Let the Christian man, then, conform his prayers to this rule in order that they may be in common and embrace all who are his brothers in Christ, not only those whom he at present sees and recognizes as such but all men who dwell on earth. For what God has determined concerning them is beyond our knowing except that it is no less godly than humane to wish and hope the best for them. Yet we ought to be drawn with a special affection to those, above others, of the household of faith, whom the apostle has particularly commended to us in everything [Gal. 6:10]. To sum up, all prayers ought to be such as to look to that community which our Lord has established in his Kingdom and his household.

39. Comparison of prayer and almsgiving

Nevertheless, this does not prevent us from praying especially for ourselves and for certain others, provided, however, our minds do not withdraw their attention from this community or turn aside from it but refer all things to it. For although prayers are individually framed, since they are directed to this end, they do not cease to be common. All this can easily be understood by a comparison. There is a general command of God's to relieve the need of all the poor, and yet those obey it who to this end succor the indigence of those whom they know or see to be suffering, even though they overlook many who are pressed by no lighter need because either they cannot know all or cannot provide for all. In this way they who, viewing and pondering this common society of the church, frame particular prayers of this sort do not resist the will of God when in their prayers, with God's people at heart, in particular terms, they commend to God themselves or others whose needs he has been pleased to make intimately known to them.

However, not all aspects of prayer and almsgiving are indeed alike. For liberality of giving can be practiced only toward those whose poverty is visible to us. But we are free to help by prayer even utterly foreign and unknown persons, however great the distance that separates them from us. This, too, is done through that general form of prayer wherein all children of God are included, among whom they also are. To this may be referred the fact that Paul urges the believers of his time to lift pure hands in every place without quarreling [1 Tim. 2:8]. In warning them that strife shuts the gate to prayers, his intention is that they offer their petitions in common with one accord.

40. "Our Father . . . in heaven"

That he is in heaven [Matt. 6:9] is added. From this we are not immediately to reason that he is bound, shut up, and surrounded, by the circumference of heaven, as by a barred enclosure. For Solomon confesses that the heaven of heavens cannot contain him [1 Kings 8:27]. And he himself says through the prophet that heaven is his seat, and the earth, his footstool [Isa. 66:1; Acts 7:49; cf. ch. 17:24]. By this he obviously means that he is not confined to any particular region but is diffused through all things. But our minds, so crass are they, could not have conceived his unspeakable glory otherwise. Consequently, it has been signified to us by "heaven," for we can behold nothing more sublime or majestic than this. While, therefore, wherever our senses comprehend anything they commonly attach it to that place, God is set beyond all place, so that when we would seek him we must rise above all perception of body and soul. Secondly, by this expression he is lifted above all chance of either corruption or change. Finally, it signifies that he embraces and holds together the entire universe and controls it by his might. Therefore it is as if he had been said to be of infinite greatness or loftiness, of incomprehensible essence, of boundless might, and of everlasting immortality. But while we hear this, our thought must be raised higher when God is spoken of, lest we dream up anything earthly or physical about him, lest we measure him by our small measure, or conform his will to our emotions. At the same time our confidence in him must be aroused, since we understand that heaven and earth are ruled by his providence and power.

To sum up: under the name "Father" is set before us that God who appeared to us in his own image that we should call upon him with assured faith. And not only does the intimate name "Father" engender trust but it is effective also to keep our minds from being drawn away to doubtful and false gods, permitting them to rise up from the only-begotten Son to the sole Father of angels and of the church. Secondly, because his throne is established in heaven, from his governing of the universe we are forcibly reminded that we do not come to him in vain, for he willingly meets us with present help. "Those who draw near to God," says the apostle, "must first believe that God exists, then that he rewards all who seek him." [Heb. 11:6 p.] Here Christ declares both of these things to his Father: that our faith rests in himself, then that we should surely be persuaded that our salvation is not overlooked by him. For he deigns to extend his providence even to us. By this elementary instruction Paul prepares us to pray properly. For before enjoining us to make our petitions known to God [Phil. 4:6], he thus prefaces the injunction: "Have no anxiety about anything" [Phil. 4:6];

"the Lord is at hand" [Phil. 4:5]. From this it is clear that those who do not feel assured that "God's eye is upon the righteous" [Ps. 34:15; cf. 1 Peter 3:12] in doubt and perplexity turn ever their prayers within their minds.

41. The first petition

The first petition is that God's name be hallowed [Matt. 6:9]; the need for it is associated with our great shame. For what is more unworthy than for God's glory to be obscured partly by our ungratefulness, partly by our ill will, and so far as lies in our power, destroyed by our presumption and insane impudence? Though all ungodly men should break out with their sacrilegious license, the holiness of God's name still shines. The prophet justifiably proclaims: "As thy name, O God, so thy praise unto all the ends of the earth" [Ps. 48:10]. For wherever God becomes known, his powers cannot fail to be manifested; might, goodness, wisdom, righteousness, mercy, truth—these should captivate us with wonderment for him, and impel us to celebrate his praise. Because, therefore, God's holiness is so unworthily snatched from him on earth, if it is not in our power to assert it, at least we are bidden to be concerned for it in our prayers.

To summarize: we should wish God to have the honor he deserves; men should never speak or think of him without the highest reverence. To this is opposed the profanity that has always been too common and even today is abroad in the world. Hence the need of this petition, which ought to have been superfluous if even a little godliness existed among us. But if holiness is associated with God's name where separated from all other names it breathes pure glory, here we are bidden to request not only that God vindicate his sacred name of all contempt and dishonor but also that he subdue the whole race of mankind to reverence for it.

Now since God reveals himself to us partly in teaching, partly in works, we can hallow him only if we render to him what is his in both respects, and so embrace all that proceeds from him. And his sternness no less than his leniency should lead us to praise him, seeing that he has engraved marks of his glory upon a manifold diversity of works, and this rightly calls forth praises from every tongue. Thus it will come about that Scripture will obtain a just authority among us, nor will anything happen to hinder us from blessing God, as in the whole course of his governance of the universe he deserves. But the petition is directed also to this end: that all impiety which has besmirched this holy name may perish and be wiped out; that all detractions and mockeries which dim this hallowing or diminish it may be banished; and that in silencing all sacrileges, God may shine forth more and more in his majesty.

42. The second petition

The second petition is: that God's Kingdom come [Matt. 6:10]. Even though it contains nothing new, it is with good reason kept separate from the first petition; for if we consider our languor in the greatest matters of all, it behooves us to extend our discussion in order to drive home something that ought to have been thoroughly known of itself. Therefore, after we have been bidden to ask God to subject and finally completely destroy everything that casts a stain upon his holy name, there is now added another similar and almost identical entreaty: that "his Kingdom come" [Matt. 6:10].

But even though the definition of this Kingdom was

put before us previously, I now briefly repeat it: God reigns where men, both by denial of themselves and by contempt of the world and of earthly life, pledge themselves to his righteousness in order to aspire to a heavenly life. Thus there are two parts to this Kingdom: first, that God by the power of his Spirit correct all the desires of the flesh which by squadrons war against him; second, that he shape all our thoughts in obedience to his rule.

Therefore, no others keep a lawful order in this petition but those who begin with themselves, that is, to be cleansed of all corruptions that disturb the peaceful state of God's Kingdom and sully its purity. Now, because the word of God is like a royal scepter, we are bidden here to entreat him to bring all men's minds and hearts into voluntary obedience to it. This happens when he manifests the working of his word through the secret inspiration of his Spirit in order that it may stand forth in the degree of honor that it deserves. Afterward we should descend to the impious, who stubbornly and with desperate madness resist his authority. Therefore God sets up his Kingdom by humbling the whole world, but in different ways. For he tames the wantonness of some, breaks the untamable pride of others. We must daily desire that God gather churches unto himself from all parts of the earth; that he spread and increase them in number; that he adorn them with gifts; that he establish a lawful order among them; on the other hand, that he cast down all enemies of pure teaching and religion; that he scatter their counsels and crush their efforts. From this it appears that zeal for daily progress is not enjoined upon us in vain, for it never goes so well with human affairs that the filthiness of vices is shaken and washed away, and full integrity flowers and grows. But its fullness is delayed to the final coming of

Christ when, as Paul teaches, "God will be all in all" [1 Cor. 15:28].

Thus this prayer ought to draw us back from worldly corruptions, which so separate us from God that his Kingdom does not thrive within us. At the same time it ought to kindle zeal for mortification of the flesh; finally, it ought to instruct us in bearing the cross. For it is in this way that God wills to spread his Kingdom. But we should not take it ill that the outward man is in decay, provided the inner man is renewed [2 Cor. 4:16]! For this is the condition of God's Kingdom: that while we submit to his righteousness, he makes us sharers in his glory. This comes to pass when, with ever-increasing splendor, he displays his light and truth, by which the darkness and falsehoods of Satan's kingdom vanish, are extinguished, and pass away. Meanwhile, he protects his own, guides them by the help of his Spirit into uprightness, and strengthens them to perseverance. But he overthrows the wicked conspiracies of enemies, unravels their stratagems and deceits, opposes their malice, represses their obstinacy, until at last he slays Antichrist with the Spirit of his mouth, and destroys all ungodliness by the brightness of his coming [2 Thess. 2:8].

43. *The third petition*

The third petition is: that God's will may be done on earth as in heaven [Matt. 6:10 p.]. Even though it depends upon his Kingdom and cannot be separated from it, still it is with reason added separately on account of our ignorance, which does not easily or immediately comprehend what it means that "God reigns in the world." It will therefore not be absurd to take it as an explanation that God will be King in the world when all submit to his will.

Here it is not a question of his secret will, by which he controls all things and directs them to their end. For even though Satan and men violently inveigh against him, he knows that by his incomprehensible plan he not only turns aside their attacks but so orders it that he may do through them what he has decreed.

But here God's other will is to be noted—namely, that to which voluntary obedience corresponds—and for that reason, heaven is by name compared to earth, for the angels, as is said in the psalm, willingly obey God, and are intent upon carrying out his commands [Ps. 103:20]. We are therefore bidden to desire that, just as in heaven nothing is done apart from God's good pleasure, and the angels dwell together in all peace and uprightness, the earth be in like manner subject to such a rule, with all arrogance and wickedness brought to an end.

And in asking this we renounce the desires of our flesh; for whoever does not resign and submit his feelings to God opposes as much as he can God's will, since only what is corrupt comes forth from us. And again by this prayer we are formed to self-denial so God may rule us according to his decision. And not this alone but also so he may create new minds and hearts in us [cf. Ps. 51:20], ours having been reduced to nothing in order for us to feel in ourselves no prompting of desire but pure agreement with his will. In sum, so we may wish nothing from ourselves but his Spirit may govern our hearts; and while the Spirit is inwardly teaching us we may learn to love the things that please him and to hate those which displease him. In consequence, our wish is that he may render futile and of no account whatever feelings are incompatible with his will.

Conclusion of the first part

Here, then, are the first three sections of the prayer. In making these requests we are to keep God's glory alone before our eyes, while leaving ourselves out of consideration and not looking to any advantage for ourselves; for such advantage, even though it amply accrues from such a prayer, must not be sought by us here. But even though all these things must nonetheless come to pass in their time, without any thought or desire or petition of ours, still we ought to desire and request them. And it is of no slight value for us to do this. Thus, we may testify and profess ourselves servants and children of God, zealously, truly, and deeply committed, to the best of our ability, to his honor. This we owe our Lord and Father. Therefore, men who do not, with this desire and zeal to further God's glory, pray that "God's name be hallowed," that "his Kingdom come," that "his will be done," should not be reckoned among God's children and servants; and inasmuch as all these things will come to pass even against such men's consent, the result will be their confusion and destruction.

3.20.44–47   Exposition of the Last Three Petitions

The last three petitions of the Lord's Prayer enable us to look to our own needs, always intending to use the benefits God gives us to show forth God's glory.

We are able to ask God for "all things in general that our bodies have need to use," assured that God's care for us extends even to "a crumb of bread and a drop of water." We ask for our "daily" bread, for "only as much as is sufficient for our need from day to day." It is by God's power alone that "life and strength are sustained" (sec. 44).

We pray for the forgiveness of our debts, our sins, knowing that we always stand in need of God's pardon and forgiveness. Yet when we pray this petition, we go on to ask that we forgive those who have "in any way injured us, either treating us unjustly in deed or insulting us in word." By praying this way, we are asking God not to forgive us unless we ourselves forgive others! (sec. 45).

The sixth petition, to deliver us from temptation, tells us that we need God's help—"not only the grace of the Spirit, to soften our hearts within and to bend and direct them to obey God, but also his aid" to enable us to withstand the assaults of evil (sec. 46).

These final three petitions show that "we especially commend to God ourselves and all our possessions" as we pray this prayer in the church with others (sec. 47).

For Reflection and Discussion

1. What does it tell us about God that God is concerned to provide for our "daily bread"? Do you pray for your "bread," daily?
2. In what ways does our willingness to forgive others relate to our prayer for God to forgive us?
3. In what ways have you experienced God "delivering" you from "evil"?

(Exposition of the last three petitions, 44–47)
44. The fourth petition

The second part of the prayer follows, in which we descend to our own affairs. We do not, indeed, bid farewell to God's glory, which as Paul testifies is to be seen even in food and drink [1 Cor. 10:31], and ask only what is expedient for us. But we have pointed out that there is this difference: God specifically claims the first three petitions and draws us wholly to himself to prove our piety in this way. Then he allows us to look after our own interests, yet under this limitation: that we seek nothing for ourselves without the intention that whatever benefits he confers upon us may show forth his glory, for nothing is more fitting than that we live and die to him [Rom. 14:7–9].

But by this petition we ask of God all things in general that our bodies have need to use under the elements of this world [Gal. 4:3], not only for food and clothing but also for everything God perceives to be beneficial to us, that we may eat our daily bread in peace. Briefly, by this we give ourselves over to his care, and entrust ourselves to his providence, that he may feed, nourish, and preserve us. For our most gracious Father does not disdain to take even our bodies under his safekeeping and guardianship in order to exercise our faith in these small matters, while we expect everything from him, even to a crumb of bread and a drop of water. For since it has come about in some way or other through our wickedness that we are affected and tormented with greater concern for body than for soul, many who venture to entrust the soul to God are still troubled about the flesh, still worry about what they shall eat, what they shall wear, and unless they have on hand abundance of wine, grain, and oil, tremble with apprehension. So much more does the shadow of this fleeting life mean to us than that everlasting immortality. Those who, relying upon God, have once for all cast out that anxiety about the care of the flesh, immediately expect from him greater things, even salvation and eternal life. It is, then, no light exercise of faith for us to hope for those things from God which otherwise cause us such anxiety. And we benefit greatly when we put off this faithlessness, which clings to the very bones of almost all men.

What certain writers say in philosophizing about "super-substantial bread" [Matt. 6:11, Vg.] seems to me to agree very little with Christ's meaning; indeed, if we did not even in this fleeting life accord to God the office of nourisher, this would be an imperfect prayer [Matt. 6:11]. The reason they give is too profane: that it is not fitting that children of God, who ought to be spiritual, not only give their attention to earthly cares but also involve God in these with themselves. As if his blessing and fatherly favor are not shown even in food, or it were written to no purpose that "godliness holds promise not only for the life to come but also for the present life" [1 Tim. 4:8 p.]! Now even though forgiveness of sins is far more important than bodily nourishment, Christ placed the inferior thing first that he might bring us gradually to the two remaining petitions, which properly belong to the heavenly life. In this he has taken account of our slowness.

But we are bidden to ask our daily bread that we may be content with the measure that our Heavenly Father has deigned to distribute to us, and not get gain by unlawful devices. Meanwhile, we must hold that it is made ours by title of gift; for, as is said in Moses, neither effort nor toil, nor our hands, acquire anything for us by themselves but by God's blessing [Lev. 26:20; cf. Deut. 8:17–18]. Indeed, not even an abundance of bread would benefit us in the slightest unless it were divinely turned into nourishment. Accordingly, this generosity of God is necessary no less for the rich than for the poor; for with full cellars and storehouses, men would faint with thirst and hunger unless they enjoyed their bread through his grace.

The word "today," or "day by day," as it is in the other Evangelist, as well as the adjective "daily," bridle the uncontrolled desire for fleeting things, with which we commonly burn without measure, and to which other evils are added. For if a greater abundance is at hand, we vainly pour it out upon pleasure, delights, ostentation, and other sorts of excess. Therefore we are bidden to ask only as much as is sufficient for our need from day to day, with this assurance: that as our Heavenly Father nourishes us today, he will not fail us tomorrow. Thus, however abundantly goods may flow to us, even when our storehouses are stuffed and our cellars full, we ought always to ask for our daily bread, for we must surely count all possessions nothing except in so far as the Lord, having poured out his blessing, makes it fruitful with continuing increase. Also, what is in our hand is not even ours except in so far as he bestows each little portion upon us hour by hour, and allows us to use it. Because the pride of man only most grudgingly allows itself to be persuaded, the Lord declares that he provided a singular proof for every age when he fed his people in the desert with manna in order to impress upon us that man does not live by bread alone but rather by the word that proceeds out of his mouth [Deut. 8:3; Matt. 4:4]. By this he shows it is by his power alone that life and strength are sustained, even though he administers it to us by physical means. So he commonly teaches us by the opposite example when he breaks, as often as he pleases, the strength of bread (and as he himself says, the staff) that those who eat may waste away with hunger [Lev. 26:26] and those who drink may be parched with thirst [cf. Ezek. 4:16–17; 14:13].

Yet those who, not content with daily bread but panting after countless things with unbridled desire, or sated with their abundance, or carefree in their piled-up riches, supplicate God with this prayer are but mocking him. For the first ones ask him what they do not wish to receive, indeed, what they utterly abominate—namely, mere daily bread—and as much as possible cover up before God their propensity to greed, while true prayer ought to pour out before him the whole mind itself and whatever lies hidden within. But others ask of him what they least expect, that is, what they think they have within themselves.

In calling the bread "ours," God's generosity, as we have said, stands forth the more, for it makes ours what is by no right owed to us [cf. Deut. 8:18]. Yet the point I also have touched upon must not be rejected: that what has been obtained by just and harmless toil is so designated, not what is got by frauds or robberies; for all that we acquire through harming another belongs to another.

The fact that we ask that it be given us signifies that it is a simple and free gift of God, however it may come to us, even when it would seem to have been obtained from our own skill and diligence, and supplied by our own hands. For it is by his blessing alone that our labors truly prosper.

45. The fifth petition

Next follows: "Forgive us our debts" [Matt. 6:12]. With this and the following petition, Christ briefly embraces all that makes for the heavenly life, as the spiritual covenant that God has made for the salvation of his church rests on these two members alone: "I shall write my laws upon their hearts," and, "I shall be merciful toward their iniquity" [Jer. 31:33 p.; cf. ch. 33:8]. Here Christ begins with forgiveness of sins, then presently adds the second grace: that God protect us by the power of his Spirit and sustain us by his aid so we may stand unvanquished against all temptations.

He calls sins "debts" because we owe penalty for them, and we could in no way satisfy it unless we were released by this forgiveness. This pardon comes of his free mercy, by which he himself generously wipes out these debts, exacting no payment from us but making satisfaction to himself by his own mercy in Christ, who once for all gave himself as a ransom [cf. Rom. 3:24]. Therefore those who trust that God is satisfied with their own or others' merits, and that by such satisfaction forgiveness of sins is paid for and purchased, share not at all in this free gift. And while they call upon God according to this form, they do nothing but subscribe to their own accusation, and even seal their condemnation by their own testimony. For they confess they are debtors unless they are released by the benefit of forgiveness, which they still do not accept but rather spurn, while they thrust their merits and satisfactions upon God. For thus they do not entreat his mercy but call his judgment.

Let those who imagine such perfection for themselves as would make it unnecessary to seek pardon have disciples whose itching ears mislead them into errors, provided it be understood that all the disciples they acquire have been snatched away from Christ, seeing that in instructing all to confess their guilt, he admits none but sinners;

not that he would foster sins by flattery, but because he knew that believers are never divested of the vices of their flesh without always remaining liable to God's judgment. We must, indeed, wish and also zealously labor that, having discharged every detail of our duty, we may truly congratulate ourselves before God as being pure from every stain. But because it pleases God gradually to restore his image in us, in such a manner that some taint always remains in our flesh, it was most necessary to provide a remedy. But if Christ, according to the authority given him by his Father, commands us throughout life to resort to prayer for the pardon of our guilt, who will tolerate these new doctors, who try to dazzle the eyes of the simple-minded with the specter of perfect innocence so as to assure them that they can rid themselves of all blame? This, according to John, is nothing else than to make God a liar [1 John 1:10]!

Also, with the same effort these rascals, by canceling one section of it, tear apart God's covenant, in which we see our salvation contained, and topple it from its foundation. Not only are they guilty of sacrilege in separating things till now joined, but also they are impious and cruel in overwhelming miserable souls with despair. Indeed, they are faithless to themselves and those like them because they induce a state of indolence diametrically opposed to God's mercy. But their objection, that in longing for the coming of God's Kingdom we at the same time seek the abolition of sin, is very childish. For in the first section of the prayer, the highest perfection is set before us, but in the latter, our weakness. Thus these two admirably accord with each other, so that, in aspiring toward the goal, we may not neglect the remedies that our necessity requires.

"As we forgive . . ."

Finally, we petition that forgiveness come to us, "as we forgive our debtors" [Matt. 6:12]: namely, as we spare and pardon all who have in any way injured us, either treating us unjustly in deed or insulting us in word. Not that it is ours to forgive the guilt of transgression or offense, for this belongs to God alone [cf. Isa. 43:25]! This, rather, is our forgiveness: willingly to cast from the mind wrath, hatred, desire for revenge, and willingly to banish to oblivion the remembrance of injustice. For this reason, we ought not to seek forgiveness of sins from God unless we ourselves also forgive the offenses against us of all those who do or have done us ill. If we retain feelings of hatred in our hearts, if we plot revenge and ponder any occasion to cause harm, and even if we do not try to get back into our enemies' good graces, by every sort of good office deserve well of them, and commend ourselves to them, by this prayer we entreat God not to forgive our sins. For we ask that he do to us as we do to others [cf. Matt. 7:12]. This, indeed, is to petition him not to do it to us unless we ourselves do it. What do people of this sort gain from their petition but a heavier judgment?

Finally, we must note that this condition—that he "forgive us as we forgive our debtors" [Matt. 6:12]—is not added because by the forgiveness we grant to others we deserve his forgiveness, as if this indicated the cause of it. Rather, by this word the Lord intended partly to comfort the weakness of our faith. For he has added this as a sign to assure us he has granted forgiveness of sins to us just as surely as we are aware of having forgiven others, provided our hearts have been emptied and purged of all hatred, envy, and vengeance. Also, it is partly by this mark that the Lord excludes from the number of his children those persons who, being eager for revenge and slow to forgive, practice persistent enmity and foment against others the very indignation that they pray to be averted from themselves. This the Lord does that such men dare not call upon him as Father. This is also eloquently expressed in Luke, in Christ's words [Luke 11:4].

46. The sixth petition

The sixth petition [Matt. 6:13], as we have said, corresponds to the promise that the law is to be engraved upon our hearts [Prov. 3:3; 2 Cor. 3:3], but because we obey God not without continual warfare and hard and trying struggles, here we seek to be equipped with such armor and defended with such protection that we may be able to win the victory. By this we are instructed that we need not only the grace of the Spirit, to soften our hearts within and to bend and direct them to obey God, but also his aid, to render us invincible against both all the stratagems and all the violent assaults of Satan. Now the forms of temptations are indeed many and varied. For wicked conceptions of the mind, provoking us to transgress the law, which either our own inordinate desire suggests to us or the devil prompts, are temptations, as are things not evil of their own nature yet which become temptations through the devil's devices, when they are so thrust before our eyes that by their appearance we are drawn away or turn aside from God [James 1:2, 14; cf. Matt. 4:1, 3; 1 Thess. 3:5]. And these temptations are either from the right or from the left. From the right are, for example, riches, power, honors, which often dull men's keenness of sight by the glitter and seeming goodness they display, and allure with their blandishments, so that, captivated by such tricks and drunk with such sweetness, men forget their God. From the left are, for example, poverty, disgrace, contempt, afflictions, and the like. Thwarted by the hardship and difficulty of these, they become despondent in mind, cast away assurance and hope, and are at last completely estranged from God.

We pray God, our Father, not to let us yield to the two sorts of temptations which, either aroused in us by our inordinate desire or proposed to us by the devil's guile, war against us. We pray, rather, that he sustain and encourage us by his hand so that, strengthened by his power, we may stand firm against all the assaults of our malign enemy, whatever thoughts he may introduce into our minds. Then we pray that whatever is presented to us tending either way we may turn to good—namely, that we may not be puffed up in prosperity or yet cast down in adversity.

Nevertheless, we do not here ask that we feel no temptations at all, for we need, rather, to be aroused, pricked, and urged by them, lest, with too much inactivity, we grow sluggish. For it is not beside the point that David wished to be tempted [cf. Ps. 26:2], and it is not without cause that the Lord daily tests his elect [Gen. 22:1; Deut. 8:2; 13:3, Vg.], chastising them by disgrace, poverty, tribulation, and other sorts of affliction. But God tries in one way, Satan in another. Satan tempts that he may destroy, condemn, confound, cast down, but God, that by proving his own children he may make trial of their sincerity, and establish their strength by exercising it; that he may mortify, purify, and cauterize their flesh, which unless it were forced under this restraint would play the wanton and vaunt itself beyond measure. Besides, Satan attacks those who are unarmed and unprepared that he may crush them unaware. God, along with the temptation, makes a way of escape, that his own may be able patiently to bear all that he imposes upon them [1 Cor. 10:13; 2 Peter 2:9].

It makes very little difference whether we understand by the word "evil" the devil or sin. Indeed, Satan himself is the enemy who lies in wait for our life [1 Peter 5:8]; moreover, he is armed with sin to destroy us. This, then, is our plea: that we may not be vanquished or overwhelmed by any temptations but may stand fast by the Lord's power against all hostile powers that attack us. This is not to succumb to temptations that, received into his care and safekeeping and secure in his protection, we may victoriously endure sin, death, the gates of hell [Matt. 16:28], and the devil's whole kingdom. This is to be freed from evil.

Here we must carefully note that it is not in our power to engage that great warrior the devil in combat, or to bear his force and onslaught. Otherwise it would be pointless or a mockery to ask of God what we already have in ourselves. Obviously those who prepare for such a combat with self-assurance do not sufficiently understand with what a ferocious and well-equipped enemy they have to deal. Now we seek to be freed from his power, as from the jaws of a mad and raging lion [1 Peter 5:8]; if the Lord did not snatch us from the midst of death, we could not help being immediately torn to pieces by his fangs and claws, and swallowed down his throat. Yet we know that if the Lord be with us, and fight for us while we keep still, "in his might we shall do mightily" [Ps. 60:12; cf. Ps. 107:14 and Comm.]. Let others trust as they will in their own capacities and powers of free choice, which they seem to themselves to possess. For us let it be enough that we stand and are strong in God's power alone.

But this prayer involves more than at first sight it presents. For if God's Spirit is our power to battle with Satan, we shall never be able to win victory until, filled with the Spirit, we cast off all weakness of our flesh. While we petition, then, to be freed from Satan and sin, we anticipate that new increases of God's grace will continually be showered upon us, until, completely filled therewith, we triumph over all evil.

To some it seems rough and harsh to ask God not to lead us into temptation, seeing that to tempt us is against his nature, as James so testifies [James 1:13]. But the question has already been partly solved, because our lust is properly the cause of all temptations that vanquish us [James 1:14], and therefore bears the blame. And James means only that it is futile and unjust to transfer to God those vices which we are compelled to impute to ourselves because we know ourselves to be guilty of them. But this does not prevent God, when it seems good to him, from turning us over to Satan, from casting us into a reprobate mind and foul desires, and from leading us into temptations, by a just but often secret judgment. For the cause has often been hidden from men, while it is certain with him. From this we gather it is not an improper expression, if we are convinced that with good reason he threatens so many times to give sure proofs of his vengeance, when he strikes the reprobate with blindness and hardness of heart.

47. The conclusion

These three petitions, in which we especially commend to God ourselves and all our possessions, clearly show what we have previously said: that the prayers of Christians ought to be public, and to look to the public edification of the church and the advancement of the believers' fellowship. For each man does not pray that something be given to him privately, but all of us in common ask our bread, forgiveness of sins, not to be led into temptation, and to be freed from evil.

Moreover, there is added the reason why we should be so bold to ask and so confident of receiving. Even though this is not extant in the Latin versions, it is so appropriate to this place that it ought not to be omitted—namely, that his "is the Kingdom, and the power, and the glory, forever" [Matt. 6:13, marg.]. This is firm and tranquil repose for our faith. For if our prayers were to be commended to God by our worth, who would dare even mutter in his presence? Now, however miserable we may be, though unworthiest of all, however devoid of all commendation, we will yet never lack a reason to pray, never be shorn of assurance, since his Kingdom, power, and glory can never be snatched away from our Father.

At the end is added, "Amen" [Matt. 6:13, marg.]. By it is expressed the warmth of desire to obtain what we have asked of God. And our hope is strengthened that all things of this sort have already been brought to pass, and will surely be granted to us, since they have been promised by God, who cannot deceive. And this agrees with the form of prayer we previously set forth: "Do, O Lord, for thy name's sake, not on account of us or our righteousness" [cf. Dan. 9:18–19]. By this the saints not only express the end of their prayers but confess themselves unworthy to obtain it unless God seeks the reason from himself, and that their confidence of being heard stems solely from God's nature.

3.20.48–49   Concluding Considerations: Adequacy of the Lord's Prayer, with Freedom to Use Other Words

Calvin contends that "we have everything we ought, or are at all able, to seek of God, set forth in this form and, as it were, rule for prayer handed down by our best Master, Christ." For, in this summary, God has "set forth what is worthy of him, acceptable to him, necessary for us—in effect, what he would willingly grant." We need add nothing to it; if we do, we are trying to supplement God's wisdom with our own and that is blasphemy. We should not stray from the Lord's Prayer since that would be holding God's will in contempt. If we do not use this prayer, we are proceeding outside faith because we are seeking our own desires apart from God's word. This is why the third-century theologian Tertullian referred to the Lord's Prayer as "the lawful prayer" (sec. 48).

Yet these prescriptions do not mean, says Calvin, that we can ever and only pray in the form of the words of the Lord's Prayer. Scripture shows us a wide variety of prayers, in all different words. What Calvin means is that no one should "ask for, expect, or demand, anything at all except what is included, by way of summary, in this prayer; and though the words may be utterly different, yet the sense ought not to vary" (sec. 49). We have great freedom in framing our prayers. But genuine prayer finds its way back to the sense and the elements we find in the Lord's Prayer.

For Reflection and Discussion
1. Why is faith a necessary ingredient for praying the Lord's Prayer?
2. When you pray in your own words, do you keep the Lord's Prayer in mind?
3. What kinds of prayers would not be reflective of the Lord's Prayer?

*(Concluding considerations: adequacy of the Lord's Prayer,
with freedom to use other words, 48–49)*

48. The Lord's Prayer is a binding rule

We have everything we ought, or are at all able, to seek of God, set forth in this form and, as it were, rule for prayer handed down by our best Master, Christ, whom the Father has appointed our teacher and to whom alone he would have us hearken [Matt. 17:5]. For he both has always been the eternal Wisdom of God [Isa. 11:2] and, made man, has been given to men, the angel of great counsel [Isa. 9:6, conflated with chapter 28:29 and Jer. 32:19].

And this prayer is in all respects so perfect that any extraneous or alien thing added to it, which cannot be related to it, is impious and unworthy to be approved by God. For in this summary he has set forth what is worthy of him, acceptable to him, necessary for us—in effect, what he would willingly grant.

For this reason, those who dare go farther and ask anything from God beyond this: first, wish to add to God's wisdom from their own, which cannot happen without insane blasphemy; secondly, do not confine themselves within God's will but, holding it in contempt, stray away farther in their uncontrolled desire; lastly, they will never obtain anything, since they pray without faith. But doubtless all such prayers are made apart from faith, for here the word of God is absent, upon which faith, if it is to stand at all, must always rely. But those who, neglecting the Master's rule, give themselves over to their own desires not only lack God's word but contend against it with all their strength. Therefore Tertullian has both truly and elegantly called it "the lawful prayer," tacitly indicating that all other prayers lie outside the law and are forbidden.

49. The Lord's Prayer does not bind us to its form of words but to its content

We would not have it understood that we are so bound by this form of prayer that we are not allowed to change it in either word or syllable. For here and there in Scripture one reads many prayers, far different from it in words, yet composed by the same Spirit, the use of which is very profitable to us. Many prayers are repeatedly suggested to believers by the same Spirit, which bear little similarity in wording. In so teaching, we mean only this: that no man should ask for, expect, or demand, anything at all except what is included, by way of summary, in this prayer; and though the words may be utterly different, yet the sense ought not to vary. Thus all prayers contained in Scripture, and those which come forth from godly breasts, are certainly to be referred to it. Truly, no other can ever be found that equals this in perfection, much less surpasses it. Here nothing is left out that ought to be thought of in the praises of God, nothing that ought to come into man's mind for his own welfare. And, indeed, it is so precisely framed that hope of attempting anything better is rightly taken away from all men. To sum up, let us remember that this is the teaching of Divine Wisdom, teaching what it willed and willing what was needful.

3.20.50–52   Special Times of Prayer and Undiscouraged Perseverance in It

Calvin suggests that in order to goad us in our "sluggishness," it is wise to "set apart certain hours for this exercise" of prayer. We also should pray in times of adversity, as well as prosperity when we will offer praise and thanksgiving to God. In all our prayers we should pray that God's will be done. In doing so, we subject our will to God's so we do not presume to try to "control God" (sec. 50).

In this stance of obedience, we give ourselves to God's providence as the expression of God's will for us. We persevere in prayer, "with desires suspended, patiently to wait for the Lord." God's answers emerge in God's time. We should not "faint or fall into despair" if God does not respond to our first requests. The Scripture shows us those who are "almost worn out with praying" and who do not cease to pray (Ps. 22:2; sec. 51).

Even in the midst of our long waiting, we know that God promises to care for us in our troubles when we pray. For "though all things fail us, yet God will never forsake us, who cannot disappoint the expectation and patience of his people." God does not always respond to the exact form of our request. But we pray in hope, relying on God's word which "will never disappoint us." Believers are sustained by this patience even as they sometimes "lie a long time in the mire" before they taste the sweetness of God. Even as we stand in hope, we continue to pray. For "unless there be in prayer a constancy to persevere, we pray in vain" (sec. 52).

For Reflection and Discussion

1. Do you set apart specific times to pray? Why or why not?
2. What have you experienced when you have had to pray for a long time before an answer to prayer has come?
3. What comfort is there in that God hears all our prayers and answers according to God's time and will?

(*Special times of prayer and undiscouraged perseverance in it,*
   50–52)
50. Prayer at regular times
But, although it has already been stated above that, lifting
up our hearts, we should ever aspire to God and pray
without ceasing, still, since our weakness is such that it has
to be supported by many aids, and our sluggishness such
that it needs to be goaded, it is fitting each one of us
should set apart certain hours for this exercise. Those
hours should not pass without prayer, and during them all
the devotion of the heart should be completely engaged in
it. These are: when we arise in the morning, before we
begin daily work, when we sit down to a meal, when by
God's blessing we have eaten, when we are getting ready
to retire.

But this must not be any superstitious observance of
hours, whereby, as if paying our debt to God, we imagine
ourselves paid up for the remaining hours. Rather, it must
be a tutelage for our weakness, which should be thus exer-
cised and repeatedly stimulated. We must take particular
care that, whenever we either are pressed or see others
pressed by any adversity, we hasten back to God, not with
swift feet but with eager hearts. Also, that we should not
let our prosperity or that of others go unnoticed, failing
to testify, by praise and thanksgiving, that we recognize
God's hand therein.

Lastly, in all prayer we ought carefully to observe that
our intention is not to bind God to particular circum-
stances, or to prescribe at what time, in what place, or in
what way he is to do anything. Accordingly, in this prayer
we are taught not to make any law for him, or impose any
condition upon him, but to leave to his decision to do
what he is to do, in what way, at what time, and in what
place it seems good to him. Therefore, before we make
any prayer for ourselves, we pray that his will be done

[Matt. 6:10]. By these words we subject our will to his in order that, restrained as by a bridle, it may not presume to control God but may make him the arbiter and director of all its entreaties.

51. *Patient perseverance in prayer*

If, with minds composed to this obedience, we allow ourselves to be ruled by the laws of divine providence, we shall easily learn to persevere in prayer and, with desires suspended, patiently to wait for the Lord. Then we shall be sure that, even though he does not appear, he is always present to us, and will in his own time declare how he has never had ears deaf to the prayers that in men's eyes he seems to have neglected. This, then, will be an ever-present consolation: that, if God should not respond to our first requests, we may not faint or fall into despair. Such is the wont of those who, carried away with their own ardor, so call upon God that unless he attends upon their first act of prayer and brings them help at once, they immediately fancy him angry and hostile toward them and, abandoning all hope of being heard, cease to call upon him. Rather, by deferring our hope with a well-tempered evenness of mind, let us follow hard upon that perseverance which Scripture strongly commends to us. For in The Psalms we can often see that David and other believers, when they are almost worn out with praying and seem to have beaten the air with their prayers as if pouring forth words to a deaf God, still do not cease to pray [Ps. 22:2]. For, unless the faith placed in it is superior to all events, the authority of God's Word does not prevail.

Also, let us not tempt God and, wearying him with our depravity, provoke him against ourselves. This is usual with many who covenant with God only under certain conditions, and, as if he were the servant of their own appetites, bind him to laws of their own stipulation. If he does not obey them at once, they become indignant, grumble, protest, murmur, and rage at him. To such, therefore, he often grants in wrath and fury what in mercy he denies to others to whom he is favorable. The children of Israel supply proof of this, for whom it would have been much better not to be heard by the Lord than to swallow his wrath with their meat [Num. 11:18, 33].

52. Unheard prayers?

But if finally even after long waiting our senses cannot learn the benefit received from prayer, or perceive any fruit from it, still our faith will make us sure of what cannot be perceived by sense, that we have obtained what was expedient. For the Lord so often and so certainly promises to care for us in our troubles, when they have once been laid upon his bosom. And so he will cause us to possess abundance in poverty, and comfort in affliction. For though all things fail us, yet God will never forsake us, who cannot disappoint the expectation and patience of his people. He alone will be for us in place of all things, since all good things are contained in him and he will reveal them to us on the Day of Judgment, when his Kingdom will be plainly manifested.

Besides, even if God grants our prayer, he does not always respond to the exact form of our request but, seeming to hold us in suspense, he yet, in a marvelous manner, shows us our prayers have not been vain. This is what John's words mean: "If we know that he hears us whenever we ask anything of him, we know that we have obtained the requests we asked of him" [1 John 5:15 p.]. This seems a diffuse superfluity of words, but the declaration is especially useful because God, even when he does not comply with our wishes, is still attentive and kindly to our prayers, so that hope relying upon his word will never disappoint us. But believers need to be sustained by this patience, since they would not long stand unless they relied upon it. For the Lord proves his people by no light trials, and does not softly exercise them, but often drives them to extremity, and allows them, so driven, to lie a long time in the mire before he gives them any taste of his sweetness. And, as Hannah says, "He kills and brings to life; he brings down to hell and brings back" [1 Sam. 2:6 p.]. What could they do here but be discouraged and rush into despair if they were not, when afflicted, desolate, and already half dead, revived by the thought that God has regard for them and will bring an end to their present misfortunes? Nevertheless, however they stand upon the assurance of that hope, they do not meanwhile cease to pray, for unless there be in prayer a constancy to persevere, we pray in vain.